# A Biblical Analysis of Corrective Church Discipline

# A Biblical Analysis of Corrective Church Discipline

## God's Loving Plan to Rescue & Restore Believers

Todd M. Fink

# A Biblical Analysis of
# Corrective Church Discipline

by
Todd M. Fink

Published by Selah Book Press

ISBN- 10: 1-944601-22-8
ISBN-13: 978-1-944601-22-5

First Edition

Scripture in bold is emphasis added by the author.

# ABBREVIATIONS

| | |
|---|---|
| NASB | New American Standard Bible |
| ESV | English Standard Version |
| NIV | New International Version |
| NKJV | New King James Version |
| NET | New English Translation |

# Table of Contents

# Chapter 1

## Introduction

## A Biblical Approach

Thank you for taking the time to read this book and for caring about this doctrine.

To begin with, my utmost desire in writing this book is to let God's Word say what it means about corrective church discipline. I want to be completely honest with Scripture and let it speak for itself, instead of making it say what I want it to say. Therefore, this book will be deeply biblical and full of Scripture. It's designed to examine God's Word and let Him speak for Himself. So please don't just skim over the Bible verses in this book, but carefully ponder them and allow God to speak to you through His divine Word.

My research to discover God's heart and will regarding corrective church discipline has led me to the conclusion that much of what has been written on this topic takes a soft and unbiblical approach. I believe this is so because it's probably the most challenging task of a church and its leaders. It's often time-consuming, ugly, has fallout, and usually involves criticism. Therefore, rather than deal with the difficulties of implementing church discipline, we often look for ways to get around it so we don't have to deal with the problems it might entail.

This might be an easier approach, but it's not the biblical approach. This book tackles this important

its not easier in the end when yur reap the fruit + consequences of your own way us- gods way doctrine head-on and seeks to let God say what He intended to say about corrective church discipline. After all, He is the one who spoke about it in the first place.

## Corrective Church Discipline Is God's Idea, Not Ours

Now while many in Christianity today don't believe or practice any form of corrective church discipline; nonetheless, God is the one who has raised the issue and spoken about it. It's His topic, and it's His business! Christ talks about it, the Apostle Paul speaks of it, James addresses it, and other New Testament authors deal with it as well.

We are commanded to preach the whole counsel of God, so we shouldn't pick and choose the topics we like and avoid the ones we dislike. However, it's clear today that this vital aspect of God's counsel regarding corrective church discipline is largely being neglected and rarely practiced.

## Formative and Corrective Discipline

Historically, scholars have outlined and defined two kinds of discipline that exists in a genuinely saved person's life. The first and most common is *formative discipline*, and the least common is *corrective discipline* (also known as church discipline or restorative discipline). Both formative and corrective discipline are aspects of discipleship as the word *disciple* is taken from the word *discipline*.

Formative discipline is the normal spiritual growth that should happen in a believer's life as they pursue spiritual maturity. We grow in Christ by hearing and reading God's Word, praying, being part of a local Bible-believing church, through fellowship, Bible study, small group participation, mentoring, and so forth. It's all a part of being a disciple of Christ.

Corrective discipline is the specific admonition or correction of an unrepentant believer who chooses to live in sin despite all God, and His people have done to persuade them to repent and return to Christ. Corrective church discipline takes place in the community of the church and involves warnings, counsel, correction, exhortation, and so forth with the hope to prevent or correct explicit, willful, unrepentant sin in the church.

Discipleship entails both a forward and backward-looking focus. Formative discipline encourages believers who are right with God to move forward in their journey toward spiritual maturity, and corrective discipline looks backward to seek out believers who are left behind in the process due to their involvement in sin. Corrective discipline is part of the "seeking out" aspect that rescues believers who are left behind and is an integral part of discipleship. When we

4

overlook corrective discipline, we overlook a critical element of discipleship.

Throughout this book, I will use the phrases, *corrective discipline, corrective church discipline,* and *church discipline* interchangeably. All these phrases will refer to what is commonly known by most, as simply, *church discipline.* However, when I use the phrase, *corrective discipline,* I will also be referring to the *"process"* of working with an unrepentant believer living in sin before they are actually placed in church discipline.

## Historical Use of Corrective Church Discipline

Corrective discipline was used all throughout the Old Testament in the Jewish community. The Jews were to be <u>cut-off</u> from their community and put out of the synagogue for violating certain laws and practices. This was a great fear for them. To be cut-off and barred from the life and community of the synagogue was a powerful form of corrective discipline. Therefore Nicodemus, Joseph of Arimathea, and many of the rulers did not confess Jesus openly for fear of being put out of the synagogue. *held more dearly to religion of self than the Lord Himself*

Corrective church discipline was also a significant part of virtually all Catholic and Evangelical churches throughout church history up until the last 70 or so years. Only recently have many modern-day churches done away with it. Therefore, it is not a new doctrine that needs to be discovered, but an ancient one that has been used for millenniums. We would be wise to heed this doctrine and practice and be careful of throwing it away so easily just because the modern-day winds of our culture blow a different breeze our way. *Times change, God doesn't*

## Nearly Every Organization Practices Discipline

Despite its biblical basis, the idea of corrective discipline can be controversial among Christians and churches. Even though virtually every organization or business practices it, for some reason, we think it's wrong when done in the church.

For example, a fraudulent lawyer can be debarred, an abusive player in the NBA can be fined, an employee can be dismissed, a doctor who is accused of malpractice can lose his or her medical license, a teacher can be fired, and so forth. The fact that other organizations or groups have some means of correcting or removing its members is widely accepted; however, if it's done in the church, many react negatively. *Amen so be it Thy will be done*

Chapter 1: Introduction

## Church Discipline Can Bring to the Minds of Many a Parade of Horrors

When many Christians, and even non-Christians think about church discipline, it can conjure up a sense of horror. Fred Greco states it well:

> Church Discipline—the very phrase seems to bring to the minds of most Christians a parade of horrors. It seems like our current image of church discipline is that of repressive, out-of-touch tyrants telling us everything that we may and may not do. This is not surprising when we consider the public incidents of abuse of authority both inside and outside the church. There is also the idea that church discipline appears out of touch with our modern understanding of Christian liberty, an understanding in which the individual Christian is his own judge in all matters regarding the Christian faith and the Christian life.[1]

Nonetheless, church discipline carried out in a biblical way is a pathway of blessing, restoration, healing, and deepening. It should not be viewed as negative, but as God meant it to be, something positive.

---

[1] Fred Greco, Church Discipline, www.ligonier.org/learn/articles/church-discipline/, accessed 02/18/2019.

## Speaking From Experience

I've had the privilege of serving the Lord in full-time ministry now for around 35 years. During this time, I've had to deal with a few instances of church discipline. I've also witnessed other churches either carry out church discipline or not. The consequences have been real for their choices.

Currently, I'm right in the middle of a church discipline situation as I write this book. I serve as an elder at a church in Mexico (where I serve as a long-term missionary), and we've had the unfortunate task of walking through the process of corrective church discipline. However, I praise God for the passionate devotion the rest of the leadership team has displayed in obeying God fully in this matter.

So, please understand that I'm not promoting anything I haven't done myself.

## A Sobering Thought

It sobers me up to ponder what the Apostle Paul wrote to the Corinthian Church and its leadership regarding church discipline in 2 Corinthians 2:9: *"Another reason I wrote you was to see if you would stand the test and be **obedient in everything**."* This verse relates to a restored believer who was put in discipline in 1 Corinthians 5. Because church discipline is one of the hardest tasks of a church and its leaders, it also proves their depth of obedience to God. Therefore, according to God, a lack of implementing church discipline is also a lack of obedience.

Therefore, rather than trying to soften the edges of church discipline because it's so tough to do, let's just let God speak on the issue and choose full obedience to Him rather than what we want, what our culture says, and what many in mainstream Christianity teach about this doctrine.

## Corrective Church Discipline Is Misunderstood

There is a lot of confusion and differing views regarding this biblical doctrine. However, when it's carefully looked at, it's not really that hard to understand.

Why is it so misunderstood today, and why are there so many different views on it? I believe it's due to the following three reasons:

1. Many pastors, leaders, and Christians just don't want to deal with corrective church discipline because it can be ugly, depressing, time-consuming and draining, and as a result, they look for the soft edges, so they don't have to deal with it.

*Not a true shepard leading + protecting the flock*

*if you dont fight wolves + rebuke folly you are not a shepard of God eisegesis*

**2.** We fail to look at the whole counsel of God on this topic and only use a few verses which support what we want to hear so we can avoid the issue.

**3.** We fail to use sound biblical principles of interpretation (hermeneutics) in understanding God's mind in this matter. An example of this has been the failure to understand how the original hearers would have understood Christ when He said in Matthew 18:17: *"If he refuses to listen to them, tell it to the church; and if he refuses to listen even to the church, **let him be to you as a Gentile and a tax collector.**"*

*exegesis*

The misunderstanding of Matthew 18:17, has wreaked havoc in correctly understanding the true meaning of corrective discipline. Therefore, we'll devote all of chapter 9 to discovering what Christ truly meant by this command.

## A Neglected Doctrine and Practice

Sadly, the vast majority of Evangelical churches today do not practice church discipline. Albert Mohler comments on this trend by saying:

> The decline of church discipline is perhaps the most visible failure of the contemporary church. No longer concerned with maintaining purity of confession or lifestyle, the contemporary church sees itself as a voluntary association of autonomous members, with minimal moral

accountability to God, much less to each other.[2]

Jay Adams also says the following about the lack of church discipline:

> In some ways, it seems that what Paul said to the church [Corinthian Church in 1 Cor. 5] was more severe than what he said about the incestuous son. His strong reprimand of the church for failing to exercise discipline and for having a lax attitude toward sin in their midst ought to be a trenchant warning to many churches today.[3] *Yikes*

Additionally, John MacArthur weighs in on the lack of church discipline today:

> Church discipline is vital to the spiritual health and the testimony of the church. Ignoring church discipline is the most visible and disastrous failure of the church in our time, because it conveys to the world that we're not really serious about sin.[4]

And perhaps, Steven J. Cole provides the most startling perspective of how most view church discipline today:

---

[2]Albert Mohler, *The Disappearance of Church Discipline–How Can We Recover? Part One,* 2005, AlbertMohler.com, http://www.albertmohler.com/2005/05/13/the-disappearance-of-church-discipline-how-can-we-recover-part-one, Accessed 08/21/2015.

[3] Jay Adams, *Handbook of Church Discipline* (Grand Rapids, Michigan, Zondervan, 1986), 68.

[4] John MacArthur, Grace to You Blog, February 5, 2013.

Years ago, I read about a pastor who became involved immorally with a married woman in his congregation. They each divorced their respective mates and then were married to each other in the church of which he was the pastor. The congregation turned out en masse for the wedding, giving open support. That tragic story reflects the dominant mood in the American church today, that we should show love and tolerance to those who fall into sin. That mentality is behind the push to accept practicing, unrepentant homosexuals as church members and even as pastors. Even among churches that would not condone these things, there are very few that practice biblical church discipline towards those who persist in sin.[5]

## A Low View of Sin

Today, we have a low view of the seriousness of sin! Immorality in the world is in a state of freefall and Christians aren't that far behind. Why is this so? I believe one of the reasons is that there's no longer any consequences or accountability in the church for Christians who get involved in sin. As a result, sin runs rampant and is viewed as permissible. We have cancer in our church bodies, and most are content

---

[5] Steven J. Cole, Dealing with Sinning Christians: An Overview of Church Discipline, https://bible.org/article/dealing-sinning-christians-overview-church-discipline-matthew-1815-17-1-corinthians-51-13, accessed 02/18/2019.

with allowing it to exist, or even grow.

A permissive mentality that overlooks the seriousness of sin negatively affects the health of our churches, which in turn, damages our witness to the world because sin and disobedience are viewed as acceptable, with no negative consequences.

**Final Thought** *We must live like there is heaven + hell + a righteous judge*

As you read this book, I would humbly ask you to reconsider what you understand about corrective church discipline and sincerely let God's Word guide you in this area. As mentioned, it's a very misunderstood doctrine but not really that difficult to understand if we apply sound hermeneutical principles and look at all God has said about it.

# Chapter 2

## What Is Corrective
## Church Discipline?

## Corrective Church Discipline Is Intensive Care for the Fallen

Corrective discipline can be described as a form of "intensive care" for **unrepentant believers who claim to be Christians** but are living in sin. Let me be clear; corrective discipline is **not** for unbelievers. It is also **not** for believers who repent and turn from their sins. It is only for **unrepentant believers who claim to be Christians** but choose to live in continual sin.

Corrective discipline should not be confused with a believer's everyday normal process of confession of sin and growth toward spiritual maturity. Every believer sins and falls short of full obedience and devotion to God. Therefore, in our daily lives we should simply confess our sins, ask God to forgive us, and He will cleanse us from all unrighteousness.

> *If we say that we have no sin, we are deceiving ourselves and the truth is not in us. **If we confess our sins, He is faithful and righteous to forgive us our sins and to cleanse us from all unrighteousness*** (1 John 1:8–9).

So, for clarity's sake, corrective church discipline is not for believers who fall short and confess their sins, but for a believer who willfully chooses to live in disobedience and refuses to confess their sin and repent. It's for the person who rejects listening to God and those He sends to them urging them to repent and change their behavior. Therefore, corrective church discipline is the practice of disciplining unrepentant believers who have chosen to live in sin, with the hope that they will repent and be reconciled to God and the church. It is also intended to protect other church members from the influence of sin. Matt Schmucker adds clarification: *a little leaven...*

> What is church discipline? In the narrowest sense, it is the act of excluding someone who professes to be a Christian from membership in the church and participation in the Lord's Supper for serious unrepentant sin — sin they refuse to let go of. More broadly, church discipline is the act of excluding an individual who carelessly brings disrepute onto the gospel and shows no commitment to doing otherwise.[6]

## Corrective Church Discipline Defined

In Matthew 18:15–20, we find Christ's teaching on corrective church discipline. In this passage, we see four clear steps to the process. Steps 1–3 are designed to persuade an unrepentant believer living in sin to repent and return to obedience to Christ. Step 4 is used in cases where an unrepentant believer living in sin refuses to listen and repent of their sin. **This last step is what we would define as corrective church discipline,**

---

[6] Matt Schmucker, *Something Different*, Tabletalk, March, 2009, p. 64. Used by Permission.

**or as just, church discipline**.

In order to rescue these unrepentant believers, serious measures should be undertaken to save them from destruction and devastation. It's an aspect of compassion designed by God to be exercised when all other measures fail. It's an expression of genuine love and is to be administered in a loving, but steadfast manner.

Unfortunately, rather than attempt to rescue brothers and sisters in the grips of sin, most churches today just let them go their own way in hopes they might find their way back to God and His fold. However, few ever do, and in the meantime, their sinful choices leave a wake of destruction in their own lives, and in the lives of those around them.

## Corrective Church Discipline Is True Love

One of the truest demonstrations of our love for a fallen believer is to seek to restore them back to a right relationship with God and the church.

John MacArthur speaks about how discipline is an act of love:

> Discipline is not inconsistent with love. It is lack of discipline, in fact, that is inconsistent with love. "Those whom the Lord loves He disciplines, and He scourges every son whom He receives" (Heb. 12:6). The Lord disciplines His children because He

loves them, and we will discipline our brothers and sisters in the Lord if we truly love Him and truly love them.[7] *Amen*

Jim Elliff and Daryl Wingerd also make a similar point regarding the relationship between church discipline and love:

> No church has a choice about obeying Christ, therefore our church must practice church discipline. But there is also beauty and value in disciplinary action that we may not immediately see. It is beautiful because it is about love. Our discipline toward a professing Christian in sin may be the most loving act he has ever experienced. However uninviting or difficult discipline might be, and however severely we must act, God has made church discipline valuable because it will either produce a holier life or a holier church, or both, when carried out obediently and harmoniously.[8] *unity*
> *one Body*
> *one mind*
> *one Spirit*

God wants the church to cooperate with Him in rescuing a believer living in unrepentant sin and see them restored in their relationship to Him and the church fellowship. If we truly love believers who have fallen into sin, and if we truly believe that sin brings death and destruction, then we will cooperate with

---

[7] John MacArthur, *1 Corinthians*, Moody, 1984, p. 125.

[8] Jim Elliff and Daryl Wingerd, *Restoring Those Who Fall*, Christian Communicators, www.CCWtoday.org, 2006, p. 18

God in exercising corrective church discipline so we can rescue and restore fallen believers.

When we stand by and allow a fallen believer to destroy their lives, damage the testimony of the church and Christ, and do nothing, I don't believe that's true love. It might appear like love, but it allows destruction, not restoration, and how can allowing destruction be defined as love?

We cannot say we love a believer caught in sin if we choose not to implement church discipline. In essence, when we don't exercise church discipline, we are saying by our actions that we do not love a sinning believer and we don't really care about him or her.

Randy Smith sums up how exercising church discipline is true love: "It's clearly foolish to say discipline is unloving. And it's clearly foolish to say because a church practices church discipline as commanded that they know nothing about forgiveness."[9]

---

[9] Randy Smith, *Sermon, Severity, Sorrow and Satan*, 2 Corinthians 2:5-11, February 23, 2014. http://jerseygrace.org/sermon/severity-sorrow-and-satan/ Accessed 02/09/2019.

## Corrective Church Discipline Is an Aspect of Discipleship

Most Christians would not associate church discipline with discipleship, but they are closely related. Discipleship entails both a forward and backward-looking focus. It encourages believers who are right with God to move forward in their journey toward spiritual maturity, and it looks backward to seek out believers who are left behind in the process due to their involvement in sin. Church discipline is part of the "seeking out" aspect that rescues believers who are left behind and is an integral part of discipleship. When we overlook church discipline, we overlook a critical aspect of discipleship.

## Corrective Church Discipline Is Important to God

Following are seven purposes for corrective church discipline and why it's so important to God (we will elaborate on these in more detail in chapter 6):

1. It promotes and protects God's holiness (Ezek. 36:16–21; 1 Cor. 5:1–5).

2. It maintains the standards and faithful witness of Christ's Church to a watching world (Matt. 5:13–16).

3. It protects the purity of the church and keeps sin from spreading throughout its ranks (Josh. 7:3; 1 Cor. 5:6–7).

4. It restores a fellow believer caught in sin and helps them find their way back to God (2 Cor. 2:6–8).

5. It prevents unrepentant believers living in sin from severe judgment (1 Cor. 5:5; 1 Cor. 11:30).

6. It warns other believers to be fearful of sinning (1 Tim. 5:19–20).

7. It tests the obedience level of a church and its leadership (2 Cor. 2:9).

## Corrective Discipline Prevents a Multitude of Sins

James 5:19-20, sums up the purpose of corrective discipline perfectly: *"My brethren, if any among you strays from the truth and one turns him back, let him know that he who turns a sinner from the error of his way **will save his soul from death and will cover a multitude of sins**."* As this verse clarifies, when we exercise corrective discipline in the life of a believer living in unrepentant sin, we save their souls from death. We also save them, and those around them, from a multitude of sins.

## Corrective Discipline Seeks to Rescue and Restore

Rescuing a fallen believer is the same principle found in the parable of the lost sheep: *"What man among you, if he has a hundred sheep and **has lost one of them**, does not leave the ninety-nine in the open pasture and go after the one which is lost **until he finds it? When he**

*has found it, he lays it on his shoulders, rejoicing"*
(Luke 15:4–5).

Christ certainly didn't leave lost sheep to fend for themselves, hoping they would stumble back to the Shepherd and His fold. Instead, He sought the lost sheep, and that's exactly what we should do with the lost sheep in our churches who are living in unrepentant sin. We should seek to rescue them by following each step of the corrective church discipline process that our loving Lord Jesus gave us in Matthew 18:15–20.

## Leading Voices on Corrective Church Discipline

J. Hampton Keathley III states:

> Though church discipline appears unloving and harsh, it nevertheless rests upon the divine authority of Scripture and is vital to the purity, power, progress, and purpose of the church.[10]

> The responsibility and necessity for discipline is not an option for the church if it obeys the Word of God, but a church must be equally concerned that Scripture is carefully followed in the practice of church discipline.[11]

---

[10] J. Hampton Keathley III, *Church Discipline*, Bible.org, https://bible.org/article/church-discipline, Accessed 10/08/2015.
[11] Ibid., Accessed 10/08/2015.

John MacArthur affirms:

> The purpose of church discipline is the spiritual restoration of fallen members and the consequent strengthening of the church and glorifying of the Lord. When a sinning believer is rebuked, and he turns from his sin and is forgiven, he is won back to fellowship with the body and with its head, Jesus Christ.[12]

Mark Dever weighs in and says:

> What is church discipline? In broad terms, church discipline is one part of the discipleship process, the part where we correct sin and point the disciple toward the better path. To be discipled is, among other things, to be disciplined. And a Christian is disciplined through instruction and correction, as in a math class where a teacher teaches the lesson and then corrects the students' errors.[13]

Curtis Thomas provides more valuable insight into church discipline as well:

> Church discipline has as its objective to recover the brother to a position of obedience, to protect the

---

[12] John MacArthur, Grace to You, *Church Discipline,* www.gty.org/resources/distinctives/DD02/church-discipline, accessed 10/08/2015.

[13] Mark Dever, *Church Discipline: How the Church Protects the Name of Jesus*, Crossway, Wheaton, IL., 2012, p. 27

integrity of the name of Christ, to purify the church, to deter sin in the congregation and to reconcile the brother to the body.[14]

And lastly, Derek Prime and Alistair Begg state:

Church discipline is neither popular nor a common practice in the church, and this is to be regretted. Its absence indicates that people have lost sight of the love and tenderness that is always to be behind it and of its necessity if those who err are to be restored.[15]

## Conclusion

Corrective church discipline can be described as a form of "intensive care" for **unrepentant believers who claim to be Christians** but are living in sin.

It has seven purposes, which shows us that the restoration of a believer living in sin is just one of the reasons for church discipline. God's holiness, the witness of His Church and its purity, the need to warn others about the dangers and consequences of sin, and the test of the obedience level of a church and its leadership are other reasons for church discipline.

Unfortunately, church discipline is largely misunderstood and rarely practiced today. This is often

---

[14] Curtis Thomas, Life in the Body of Christ, Founders Press, 2006, p. 218

[15] Derek Prime and Alistair Begg, *On Being a Pastor*, Moody Press, 2004, p. 228

because we tend to look for a way out of doing it as it's difficult and often ugly. Nonetheless, church discipline rests upon the divine authority of Scripture and is an act of love.

James 5:19–20, summarizes so perfectly its purpose: *"My brethren, if any among you strays from the truth and one turns him back, let him know that he who turns a sinner from the error of his way **will save his soul from death and will cover a multitude of sins.**"*

# Chapter 3

## The Old Testament and Corrective Discipline

## Corrective Discipline in the Old Testament

We see a valuable example of how God used corrective discipline in the Old Testament. When the nation of Israel would fall away from God, He would punish them with the hope that they would return to Him. We see this cycle over and over again in the book of Judges, in 1 and 2 Samuel, in 1 and 2 Kings, and the Major and Minor Prophets.

Things got so bad in the nation of Israel that the Northern Kingdom (known as Israel) was taken into captivity and deported to Assyria in 722 BC. Then, later, the Southern Kingdom (known as Judah) was taken into captivity and deported to Babylon in 586 BC.

The Northern Kingdom would never return to Israel again, and are therefore called, "The 10 Lost Tribes of Israel." The Southern Kingdom spent 70 years in captivity, and only a portion of them returned to Israel.

These deportations and the destruction of Jerusalem (their capital city), were horrific and deadly events. Here's just one verse about God's punishment for His wayward children in the Old Testament: *"And though they go into captivity before their enemies, from there I will command the sword that it slay them, **and I will set My eyes against them for evil and not for good**"* (Amos 9:4). What a sad state of affairs! The nation of Israel could have had such rich blessings, but instead, they chose sin and rebellion. It's the same for us today: obedience brings blessings; disobedience brings death and destruction.

God's heart in disciplining His wayward people was to save them from death and destruction. It was love in its truest sense.

## The Purpose of Corrective Discipline in the Old Testament

We see the principle of corrective discipline in the Old Testament in the commands given by God to the nation of Israel to discipline and punish sin among them. Punishment ranged from death by stoning for large offenses, and less punishment for sins such as stealing and lying. We also see that in some cases, because of rebellion or lack of obedience to God's laws, individuals were excommunicated (cut off) from being a part of God's chosen people.

We repeatedly see that one of God's purposes for corrective discipline was to maintain a holy and separate people so they would have a greater impact to reveal God and His love to the world: *"Now then, if you will indeed obey My voice and keep My covenant, then you shall be My own possession among all the peoples, for all the earth is Mine; and you shall be to Me a **kingdom of priests and a holy nation**"* (Ex. 19:5–6). When the nation of Israel, or individuals were involved in sin, it diminished, or removed altogether, God's purpose for them to be a kingdom of priests and a holy nation.

Corrective discipline was also used by God because of His love for them, as the wages of sin bring death to any generation, so God in His love desired to protect them from sin and the destruction it brings.

## Corrective Discipline Defined in the Old Testament

Following are several verses that speak of corrective discipline in the Old Testament:

- *"But an uncircumcised male who is not circumcised in the flesh of his foreskin, that person shall be **cut off** from his people; he has broken My covenant"* (Gen. 17:14).

- *"Seven days you shall eat unleavened bread, but on the first day you shall remove leaven from your houses; for whoever eats anything leavened from the first day until the seventh day, that person shall be **cut off** from Israel"* (Ex. 12:15).

- *"Therefore, you are to observe the Sabbath, for it is holy to you. Everyone who profanes it shall surely be put to death; for whoever does any work on it, that person shall be **cut off** from among his people"* (Ex. 31:14).

The phrase, **cut off**, is used 22 times in just the books of Exodus and Leviticus. So, as we can see repeatedly, a Jew who disobeyed key commandments of God's Law was to be cut off from Israel.

This phrase, *cut off,* means to be removed from, separated from, cast out, ostracized, shunned, or banned. Also, in more serious cases, it meant death by stoning.

## Fear of Being Put Out of the Synagogue

A large part of corrective discipline in the Jewish community involved being put out of the synagogue for refusing to repent of sin, not obeying certain laws and practices, and for believing or teaching false doctrine.

To be put out of the synagogue was disastrous for a Jew. It meant they lost their spiritual connection, their social connection, their business connection, their educational connection, their school connection for their children (the synagogue is where the education of children and youth took place), and on some occasions, their family connection.

Therefore, many of the Jews in Jesus' day did not openly confess Him for fear of being put out of the synagogue: *"Nevertheless many even of the rulers believed in Him, but because of the Pharisees they were not confessing Him, **for fear that they would be put out of the synagogue**"* (John 12:42).

The Gentiles, along with Jewish sinners and tax collectors, were all banned from the synagogue and cut-off from the Jewish community.

## Conclusion

As we can see, God exercised nationwide corrective discipline on a large scale, and individually as well, all throughout the Old Testament. He did this because of His great love for them, and so that they would be a kingdom of priests and a holy nation in order to broadcast to the whole world who God was and how He desired us to live. This same theme is carried over into the New Testament as well.

We can biblically state, then, that when a church exercises corrective church discipline, it is doing what God did all throughout the Old Testament.

# Chapter 4

## Jesus and Corrective Church Discipline

## Old Testament Corrective Discipline Carried Over to the New Testament

This principle of dealing with sin among God's people is carried into the New Testament and has application to the church and believers today as well. God chooses to discipline believers living in sin in order to force them to return to Him, and He uses the church to be His vehicle to carry this out. Sometimes this works, sometimes it doesn't (like the nation of Israel). Nonetheless, it is commanded and is, unfortunately, the last resort in a believer's life who is living in rebellion and disobedience to God with no willingness to repent and be restored.

Once again, it should be noted that church discipline is only reserved for unrepentant believers who call themselves Christians and not for non-believers. They are distinct groups and are dealt with differently according to God's Word. Also, unlike the Old Testament, the church today does not carry out punishment in the sense of stoning and applying criminal charges. This is left up to governments and God to apply.

### Jesus Speaks

Matthew 18:15–20, is one of the first mentions of corrective church discipline in the New Testament. In this passage, we see more of the process for church discipline, and in 1 Corinthians 5, and other New

Testament verses, we see more of the application of it.
Now let's look at what Christ said and what He
outlined for the corrective discipline process to entail:

> *If your brother sins, go and show him his fault in
> private; if he listens to you, you have won your brother.
> But if he does not listen to you, take one or two more
> with you, so that by the mouth of two or three witnesses
> every fact may be confirmed. If he refuses to listen to
> them, tell it to the church; and if he refuses to listen
> even to the church, let him be to you as a Gentile and a
> tax collector. Truly I say to you, whatever you bind on
> earth shall have been bound in heaven; and whatever
> you loose on earth shall have been loosed in heaven.
> Again, I say to you, that if two of you agree on earth
> about anything that they may ask, it shall be done for
> them by My Father who is in heaven. For where two or
> three have gathered together in My name, I am there in
> their midst.*

## Clear Commands

Notice in this passage the number of verbs Christ
used. Each of these verbs is a direct command we are
told to follow. Let's take note of them for a moment:

1. *If your brother sins,* **go and show** *him his fault.*

2. *But if he does not listen to you,* **take one or two
   more with you.**

3. *If he refuses to listen to them,* **tell it to the church.**

4. *If he refuses to listen even to the church,* **let him be to you** *as a Gentile and a tax collector.*

We see four direct action verbs in this passage which are clear commands given by Christ. Each command is built upon the previous one and is more severe in nature. These commands, in and of themselves alone, should cause us to reconsider if we are neglecting the process of corrective church discipline.

## Jesus' Procedure for Corrective Church Discipline

Jesus gives us a very specific procedure to follow when attempting to restore a fellow believer who is caught in sin. He outlines four steps to follow:

1. Go and show your brother his fault in private, seeking restoration (Matt. 18:15).

2. If this person refuses to respond to your private admonition, involve one or two other trusted, mature Christians so that every fact may be confirmed (Matt. 18:16).

3. If this person still refuses to listen and turn from their sin, bring the matter to the church leaders so they can tell it to the church. In so doing, the faithful from the church can go to this person and try to convince them to turn from their sin as well.

4. If this person refuses to listen to the church,

then they are to be treated as a **Gentile and tax collector** (because this command is so key to understanding church discipline, and because it's so misunderstood today, we'll devote chapter 9 to discovering its true biblical meaning).

In order to carry out these steps, we must care enough to lovingly speak the truth, even when we would rather gloss over a problem or ignore an issue.

Later, in chapter 7, we will look more in-depth at these four steps that should guide us in the church discipline process.

## The Meaning of "Where Two or Three Are Gathered"

This is probably one of the most misunderstood and misquoted verses in the Bible. Correctly understanding Scripture will only happen as we look at the full context in which verses are found. The topic at hand in this context is church discipline, not Bible studies or prayer meetings. God promises that when we put someone in church discipline, and we pray for Him to bind and loose certain things regarding church discipline, that He is with us in the process. Amen

## Conclusion

Jesus carried over the idea of Old Testament corrective discipline into the New Covenant. He is the one who led the way and introduced the doctrine in the New Testament. He gave us four clear steps we are commanded to follow, and He gave each believer the command to participate in the process when they see blatant sin by other believers in their midst. According to Christ, corrective discipline is not an option, but a command to be obeyed when we see a believer living in unrepentant sin.

Jesus has chosen to give each believer, and the church, the privilege, and responsibility of joining Him in this important matter of church discipline. He promises to participate and move from heaven in a unique way and needs each believer, and the church, to act responsibly in order for Him to fully work in the life of an unrepentant believer. Therefore, He says: *"Truly I say to you,* **whatever you bind on earth shall have been bound in heaven; and whatever you loose on earth shall have been loosed in heaven.** *Again, I say to you, that if two of you agree on earth about anything that they may ask, it shall be done for them by My Father who is in heaven.* **For where two or three have gathered together in My name, I am there in their midst"** (Matt. 18:18–20).

# Chapter 5

## The New Testament and Corrective Church Discipline

## The New Testament Speaks

Not only do we have the Old Testament and Jesus speaking on the issue of corrective church discipline, but many other New Testament authors, under the inspiration of the Holy Spirit, speak out as well. Once again, church discipline is God's idea, not ours. Therefore, let's hear Him speak as we look at the following verses that deal, in some way or another, with the issue of church discipline.

## 1 Corinthians 5

This chapter is the clearest case of what corrective church discipline looks like in the New Testament. Therefore, please read it slowly and carefully in order to understand God's will and purpose for it:

*"It is actually reported that there is immorality among you, and immorality of such a kind as does not exist even among the Gentiles, that someone has his father's wife.* **You have become arrogant and have not mourned instead, so that the one who had done this deed would be removed from your midst.** *For I, on my part, though absent in body but present in spirit, have already judged him who has so committed this, as though I were present. In the name of our Lord Jesus, when you are assembled, and I with you in spirit, with the power of our Lord Jesus, I have decided to* **deliver such a one to Satan for the destruction of his flesh,** *so that his spirit may be saved in the day of the Lord Jesus. Your boasting is not good. Do*

*you not know that a little leaven leavens the whole lump of dough? Clean out the old leaven so that you may be a new lump, just as you are in fact unleavened. For Christ, our Passover also has been sacrificed. Therefore, let us celebrate the feast, not with old leaven, nor with the leaven of malice and wickedness, but with the unleavened bread of sincerity and truth. I wrote you in my letter not to associate with immoral people; I did not at all mean with the immoral people of this world, or with the covetous and swindlers, or with idolaters, for then you would have to go out of the world. But actually, I wrote to you* **not to associate with any so-called brother** *if he is an immoral person, or covetous, or an idolater, or a reviler, or a drunkard, or a swindler –* **not even to eat with such a one**. *For what have I to do with judging outsiders? Do you not judge those who are within the church? But those who are outside, God judges.* **Remove the wicked man from among yourselves.**"

This chapter begins with a rebuke to the Corinthian Church because there was a lack of grief among them regarding sin in their midst. Instead of being concerned, they were passive and even proud that the situation was not dealt with openly.

Maybe they had the idea that they were just supposed to accept everyone and love them regardless of their sin. Maybe they confused how we treat and love an unbeliever and how we treat a member of the body of Christ who willfully disobeys and commits sin, or maybe they didn't believe in corrective church discipline altogether? Whatever their thinking was, there was a lack of concern, a sense of passivity, and even boasting about not dealing with sin in their midst. For these ungodly attitudes, they were strongly rebuked.

We then see a biblical principle found in the Old Testament transferred to this New Testament passage. God is concerned about purity among His people so that sin doesn't spread and infect others: "*Your boasting is not good.* **Do you not know that a little leaven leavens the whole lump of dough?** *Clean out the old leaven so that you may be a new lump, just as you are in fact unleavened*" (1 Cor. 5:6–7). This principle harmonizes with God's dealings in the Old Testament to maintain purity and obedience among His people.

We also see this same principle in governments as they punish crimes. If our government was passive about dealing with sin and putting criminals in prison, I fear to think of what our country would look like. If even governments deal with sin, how much more should Christ's church? The church should be the first to call out sin and discipline those who call themselves believers yet are living in sin.

In this passage (1 Cor. 5), it is mentioned three times to put this unrepentant believer out of their midst. It is also mentioned that there was to be no association with them as long as they remained in their unrepentant state. *bear fruits in keeping w/ repentance!*

Notice also in this passage that we are given a clear command to hold accountable (Scripture uses the word, *judge*) those within the church who are living in sin. Once again, look carefully at what God says here:

*"But now I am writing to you that **you must not associate with anyone who claims to be a brother** or sister but is sexually immoral or greedy, an idolater or slanderer, a drunkard or swindler. **Do not even eat with such people.** What business is it of mine to judge those outside the church? **Are you not to judge those inside?** God will judge those outside. '**Expel the wicked person from among you**'"* (1 Cor. 5:11–13).

Contrary to what some might believe, God clearly commands us to <u>hold accountable</u> (judge) believers in the church who are living in unrepentant sin. This entails removing them from our midst and not associating with them. It is designed by God to <u>apply pressure</u> in their lives with the hope that they will repent and be restored. It's love in action attempting to rescue and restore.

## 2 Corinthians 2:6–9

Most Bible scholars agree that this passage shows the results of the church discipline that was implemented on the unrepentant believer in 1 Corinthians 5. After repenting, he was welcomed back into the Corinthian Church.

*"The punishment inflicted on him by the majority is sufficient. Now instead, you ought to forgive and comfort him, so that he will not be overwhelmed by excessive sorrow. I urge you, therefore, to reaffirm your love for him. Another reason I wrote you was to see if you would stand the test and be obedient in everything."*

Some believe church discipline is not necessary or doesn't work. This passage proves otherwise. Church discipline worked beautifully, and this brother was restored to Christ and the church as a result.

One of the great misunderstandings of our day is that church discipline is harsh and cold. It is true that in some situations it has been applied this way by some churches. However, the biblical model is the loving discipline of a child of God so that they can be saved from the destruction their sin will cause them, the name of Christ, the church, their family, and loved ones. Sin always affects others and is not limited to just one individual.

The lack of corrective discipline is like a group of people watching a person in a boat about to go over a waterfall to their death while standing by and doing nothing. This action has no resemblance whatsoever of biblical love.

Others believe we should just love people regardless of their sin. This is true, but love has more than one side, and it's important to distinguish how love is applied to non-believers and believers. For non-believers in sin, we do what Christ did on earth; we eat and drink with them, love and accept them, and teach them God's commands so that they will turn to Christ and His will for them. However, for believers who choose to live in unrepentant sin after knowing the truth, we apply love to them in the form of church discipline in order to turn them from their sin.

For the non-believer, knowledge of right and wrong is what they need, but for the believer who has this knowledge and yet chooses to continue living in sin, church discipline is what they need. God calls upon His church to exercise church discipline to those in the body of Christ who are living in sin, so they will stop their destructive ways and save themselves, and others around them, from sin's death and consequences.

## Galatians 6:1

*"Brethren, even if anyone is caught in any trespass, you who are spiritual, **restore such a one in a spirit of gentleness**; each one looking to yourself, so that you too will not be tempted."*

One of the ways we can measure our spiritual maturity is whether we have a heart to restore believers caught in sin or not. For those who do not believe in corrective discipline, it reveals a lack of spiritual maturity and love for fallen believers. Allowing an unrepentant believer to live in their sin is not love, as the wages of sin is death (Rom. 3:23).

## 2 Thessalonians 3:14–15

*"Take special note of anyone who does not obey our instruction in this letter. **Do not associate with them**, in order that they may feel ashamed. Yet do not regard them as an enemy, but warn them as you would a fellow believer."*

For those unwilling to obey clear commands of Scripture, as was the case with some in the church in Thessalonica, Paul gave a strong command not to associate with them so they would feel ashamed. This situation seems to have some relation to corrective discipline as the reason given for not associating with a believer unwilling to obey God's Word was so that they would feel ashamed.

## 1 Timothy 5:19–21

*"Do not receive an accusation against an elder except on the basis of two or three witnesses. Those who continue in sin, **rebuke in the presence of all**, so that the rest also will be **fearful of sinning**. I solemnly charge you in the presence of God and of Christ Jesus and of His chosen angels, to maintain these principles without bias, doing nothing in a spirit of partiality."*

because sin has no place
amongst God's people

46

Here we see a form of church discipline applied to church leaders who continue to sin in some area. They are to be rebuked in front of the whole church, so the rest will be fearful of sinning.

## 2 Timothy 3:1–5

*"But realize this, that in the last days difficult times will come. For men will be lovers of self, lovers of money, boastful, arrogant, revilers, disobedient to parents, ungrateful, unholy, unloving, irreconcilable, malicious gossips, without self-control, brutal, haters of good, treacherous, reckless, conceited, lovers of pleasure rather than lovers of God,* **holding to a form of godliness***, although they have denied its power;* **avoid such men as these***."*

Interestingly, this passage ends with a claim that these attitudes were being displayed, in some part, by those *"holding to a form of godliness."* Some would say that these are people who claim to be believers but are living in the flesh. Others would say they are unbelievers who think they are saved but are not. Regardless of our interpretation, these people who *"hold to a form of godliness"* but display ungodly attitudes habitually, are to be avoided.

## 2 Thessalonians 3:6

*"Now we command you, brethren, in the name of our Lord Jesus Christ, that you* **keep away** *from every brother*

*who leads an **unruly life** and not according to the tradition which you received from us."*

Sometimes we only believe church discipline applies to sexual or severely gross sins. However, being unruly, which can be defined as disorderly, disruptive, and unwilling to be under authority or the control of the church leadership, applies as well.

### Titus 3:10–11

*"Warn a divisive person once, and then warn him a second time. After that, **have nothing to do with him**. You may be sure that such a man is warped and sinful; he is self-condemned."*

Here we see a strong message being sent by God regarding how we are to treat divisive people. Divisive people are those who look for ways to stir up hostility, anger, rumors, gossip, and disagreement among others.

Regarding doctrinal issues that can be divisive, it should be noted that not all who are striving to be biblical should be considered divisive. The prophets, Jesus, and the apostles all caused division when it came to theological matters. However, we should be gracious and respectful in doctrinal matters, not being rude or inappropriately divisive (2 Tim. 2:24–26). We can be right, but at the same time, not rude and divisive.

## James 5:19–20

*"My brothers, if one of you should wander from the truth and someone should bring him back, remember this:* **Whoever turns a sinner from the error of his way will save him from death and cover over a multitude of sins.***"*

We often forget that being passive regarding sin in the life of a believer only brings death and a multitude of sins. There is nothing healthy about this at all! We should realize that God's solution to this issue is corrective discipline. *He shows us the way we must trust + walk in it.*

## Lessons From the Letters to the Seven Churches

Interestingly, we see in the letters to the seven churches in the book of Revelation two key issues that concerned Jesus the most about His Church. These are vital to understand. The first is the allowance of false doctrine, and the second is the allowance of sin in the church.

## 1. Matters Regarding False Doctrine in the Church

Revelation 2:14–16: *"But I have a few things against you, because you have there some **who hold the teaching of Balaam**, who kept teaching Balak to put a stumbling block before the sons of Israel, to eat things sacrificed to idols and to commit acts of immorality. So you also have some **who in the same way hold the teaching of the Nicolaitans**. Therefore repent; or else I am coming to you* quickly, and I will make war against them with the sword of My mouth."

Here we see a great concern Jesus has for false doctrine in the church. Christ commanded this church to repent or He would come and make war with them. These are strong words which reveal Christ's attitude toward false doctrine in His Church!

Revelation 2:24: *"But I say to you, the rest who are in Thyatira, **who do not hold this teaching**, who have not known the deep things of Satan, as they call them — I place no other burden on you."* Once again, we see Christ's concern for false doctrine in the church.

## 2. Matters Regarding Sin in the Church

Revelation 2:20–23: *"But I have this against you, that you tolerate the woman Jezebel, who calls herself a prophetess, and **she teaches and leads My bond-servants astray so that they commit acts of immorality and eat things sacrificed to idols**. I gave her time to repent, and she does not want to repent of her immorality. Behold, I will **throw her on a bed of sickness, and those who commit adultery with her into great tribulation**, unless they repent of her deeds. And **I will kill her children with pestilence**, and all the churches will know that I am He who searches the minds and hearts; and I will give to each one of you according to your deeds."*

In this passage, we see false teaching that led to acts of immorality. Christ took these sins so seriously that

bad doctrine → bad living

He threw Jezebel on a bed of sickness, threw those who committed adultery with her into great tribulation, and killed the children of Jezebel with pestilence. This reveals how seriously Christ takes sin in the church and how it grieves Him deeply when He finds it within our ranks left unchecked.

## A Unified Message

All the verses in the New Testament dealing with how we should treat unrepentant believers living in sin all have the same message; we are to use corrective discipline in their lives. This idea of corrective discipline harmonizes with how God dealt with unrepentant sinners in the Old Testament and what Christ taught about it as well. Corrective church discipline is biblical and, therefore, should be utilized when needed.

## Conclusion

We see that Jesus is concerned about two main factors in the church: false doctrine, and sin. Because these two areas are so vital to the health of a person and the church, they are under severe attack by Satan. Unfortunately, today doctrine is not a focus in many churches, and church discipline is practically non-existent.

When a believer is living in sin in one of these two areas and refuses to repent after we have utilized the corrective discipline process, then Scripture teaches that they are to be placed in church discipline.

John MacArthur provides this sober thought:

> Unless the public sin of a believer is dealt with publicly, people will think the church does not take sin seriously and therefore gives tacit approval of it. A church that does not discipline sinning members (including the most prominent members) loses its credibility, because it does not take seriously its own doctrines and standards.[16]

The summary of the New Testament's teaching on how we should treat unrepentant believers living in sin is clear. We are to use corrective church discipline in their lives. This means we should not associate with them (1 Cor. 5:9), we should not eat with them (1 Cor. 5:11), they are to be expelled from the church fellowship (1 Cor. 5:12–13), we should consider them as under punishment (2 Cor. 2:6), they are to feel shame (2 Thess. 3:14), we are to keep away from them (2 Thess. 3:6), and so forth. The only exception to having contact with a believer in corrective church discipline would be if it involves some movement on their part seeking to repent and be restored. This sounds harsh, but it's the biblical commands we are given.

---

[16] John MacArthur, *Galatians*, Moody, 1987, p. 57.

# Chapter 6

# What Is the Purpose of
# Corrective Church Discipline?

Many Christians, and even non-Christians, might wonder and ask, "What if we already know the person living in unrepentant sin will not repent? What possible good can come from the church discipline process?" Sadly, this question is all too often an accurate assessment of many church discipline situations. It is generally true that by the time we move to the last stage of the corrective discipline process, in most cases, the person has already made up their mind that they will not repent and obey God.

However, it's critical that we understand that corrective church discipline has more than just the one purpose of rescuing and restoring an unrepentant believer living in sin. Following are seven reasons we find in Scripture regarding the purpose of corrective church discipline and why it should be carried out even if an unrepentant believer living in sin refuses to repent or leaves the church.

## 1. It Promotes and Protects God's Holiness

Behind all that the church and believers do is the foundational concept that each believer is a saint and priest who should be reflecting their King's attributes. An unrepentant believer living in sin, and a local church who turns away from dealing with sin in their midst, severely damage their King's reputation and the purpose to which each believer has been called.

In the Old Testament we see a foundational principle of how God's people were to be a kingdom of priests and a holy nation: "*Now then, if you will indeed obey My voice and keep My covenant, then you shall be My own possession among all the peoples, for all the earth is Mine; and you shall be to Me a* **kingdom of priests and a holy nation**" (Ex. 19:5–6).

In the New Testament this concept is transferred to all believers as well: "*But you are a* **chosen race, a royal priesthood, a holy nation**, *a people for God's own possession, so that you may proclaim the excellencies of Him who has called you out of darkness into His marvelous light*" (1 Pet. 2:9).

One of the marks of a healthy Christian is that they turn away from sin. This, in turn, makes them a glowing witness for God: "*Nevertheless, God's solid foundation stands firm, sealed with this inscription: 'The Lord knows those who are his,' and, '***Everyone who confesses the name of the Lord must turn away from wickedness***'*" (2 Tim. 2:19).

Even in cases where restoration might not work because the disobedient Christian refuses to repent, church discipline must still be implemented to protect and promote God's holiness.

A believer living in unrepentant sin is a direct violation of their calling and purpose in life. Moreover, a church who refuses to discipline this sinner stains God's holiness and the purpose for His Church.

## 2. It Maintains the Standards and Faithful Witness of Christ's Church to a Watching World

In the same way the nation of Israel was supposed to be a light to the world reflecting who God is and how He desired for them to live, today, in the New Testament, the church is to be a light and example to the world as well:

> **You are the salt of the earth**; *but if the salt has become tasteless, how can it be made salty again? It is no longer good for anything, except to be thrown out and trampled underfoot by men.* **You are the light of the world**. *A city set on a hill cannot be hidden; nor does anyone light a lamp and put it under a basket, but on the lampstand, and it gives light to all who are in the house.* **Let your light shine before men in such a way that they may see your good works and glorify your Father who is in heaven** (Matt. 5:13–16).

A believer living in sin, and a local church unwilling to deal with it, drastically violate one of the main purposes to which they have been called. They also allow Satan and the world to mock them because they claim to be children of God but live like children of Satan and the world.

## 3. It Protects the Purity of the Church

An often overlooked purpose of church discipline by many is the failure to realize that one of its main objectives is to protect the rest of the church from the cancer of sin and rebellion. Yes, it does exist to rescue the unrepentant believer, which is extremely important, but again, one of its primary functions is to keep the rest of the church healthy. If sin in the church is allowed to spread, then the purity of Christ's church is affected.

Also, the destruction and pain the rest of the church can fall into by copying the behavior of an unrepentant sinner can be devastating. By exercising church discipline, we make a bold statement to the church that sin is serious and has no place in a believer's life. By not exercising church discipline, we say just the opposite.

The purity of the church seems to be the Holy Spirit's main focus when He inspired the Apostle Paul to write the following in 1 Corinthians 5:6-7: *"Your boasting is not good. Do you not know that a **little leaven leavens the whole lump of dough?** Clean out the old leaven so that you may be a new lump, just as you are in fact unleavened."*

This passage confirms that one of Paul's main concerns in the whole matter of church discipline in 1 Corinthians 5 was the purity of the church.

In this passage, God reveals three reasons why He is so concerned about purity in the church, and therefore, led Paul to exercise church discipline: (1) it protects the church from becoming contaminated by sin and its destruction (2) it rescues individual Christians from sin, and (3) it allows the church to have a greater witness to the world regarding who God is and how He desires us to live.

When sin is allowed in the lives of those claiming to be followers of Christ, God's message is damaged because the world sees no difference between how unbelievers and God's people live.

This same concern is used again regarding church leaders who fall into sin. They are to be rebuked before all so that others in the church may be fearful of sinning:

> *Do not receive an accusation against an elder except on the basis of two or three witnesses. Those who continue in sin, **rebuke in the presence of all, so that the rest also will be fearful of sinning**. I solemnly charge you in the presence of God and of Christ Jesus and of His chosen angels, to maintain these principles without bias, doing nothing in a spirit of partiality* (1 Tim. 5:19–21).

Christ is very concerned about the purity of His church; therefore, church discipline is one of God's ways to keep the church pure.

We see this same principle in Ephesians 5:

*Husbands, love your wives, just as Christ loved the church and gave himself up for her to make her holy, cleansing her by the washing with water through the word, and to present her to himself as a radiant church, **without stain or wrinkle or any other blemish, but holy and blameless.** This mystery is great; but I am speaking with reference to Christ and the church* (Eph. 5:25–27, 32).

While this passage is talking about marriage, God includes within it His desire to have a radiant church without wrinkle or any other blemish, a church that is holy and blameless. Certainly, by allowing sin to go unchecked in the church, and not exercising corrective discipline, is not keeping Christ's Church holy and blameless.

Christ also desires a pure bride that is devoted to Him with sincerity and cleanliness:

*I am jealous for you with a godly jealousy. I promised you to one husband, to Christ, so that I might present you as a **pure virgin** to him. But I am afraid that just as Eve was deceived by the serpent's cunning, your minds may somehow be led astray from **your sincere and pure devotion to Christ*** (2 Cor. 11:2–3).

Wayne Grudem sees the value of maintaining the purity of the church by stating:

Church discipline has three primary purposes. The first is to restore fallen Christians to usefulness to God and fellowship with His church. The second is to guard and preserve the honor of God. And the third purpose is to protect the purity of the church.[17]

Church discipline brings a cleansing effect on the church that is healthy. On the contrary, allowing believers to live in unrepentant sin, and doing nothing about it, allows sin to grow like cancer in a church and is not healthy.

Many pastors and Christians are reluctant to exercise church discipline thinking it will harm their churches, but just the opposite is true, it will bring health.

## 4. It Restores a Fellow Believer Caught in Sin

Church discipline can be described as a form of "intensive care" for **unrepentant believers who claim to be Christians** but are living in sin. It is **not** for non-believers. It is also **not** for believers who repent and turn from their sins. Church discipline is only for **unrepentant believers who claim to be Christians** but are living in sin.

---

[17] Wayne Grudem, Pastoral Leadership for Manhood and Womanhood, Crossway, 2002, p. 168.

Church discipline can also be defined as the practice of disciplining unrepentant believers when they have chosen to live in sin with the hope that they will repent and be reconciled to God and the church. It is also intended to protect other church members from the influence of sin.

In order to rescue these unrepentant believers, serious measures must be undertaken to save them from sin's destruction. It's an aspect of discipleship designed by God to be exercised when all other measures fail. It's an expression of genuine love and is to be administered in a loving, but steadfast manner.

Our goal in the restoration of a disobedient Christian is not simply to see a person confess their sin, but to return to their former condition of usefulness to the Lord: *"Brothers, if someone is caught in a sin, you who are spiritual should **restore** him gently. But watch yourself, or you also may be tempted. Carry each other's burdens, and in this way, you will fulfill the law of Christ"* (Gal. 6:1–2).

Restoration of an unrepentant believer living in sin is our goal. In so doing, we save this person, and all those around them, from a multitude of sins: *"My brothers, if one of you should wander from the truth and someone should bring him back, remember this: **Whoever turns a sinner from the error of his way will save him from death and cover over a multitude of sins"*** (Jam. 5:19–20).

## 5. It Protects Unrepentant Believers Living in Sin From Severe Judgment

For unrepentant believers living in sin, they run the risk of being judged severely by God. The following verses bring a sharp wake-up call to this often, overlooked reality:

> *For he who eats and drinks, eats and drinks judgment to himself if he does not judge the body rightly. **For this reason, many among you are weak and sick, and a number sleep [have died].** But if we judged ourselves rightly, we would not be judged. But when we are judged, we are disciplined by the Lord so that we will not be condemned along with the world* (1 Cor. 11:29–32).

This passage talks about believers who were living in unrepentant sin but were participating in the Lord's Supper as if everything was okay. Because of sin in their lives, God caused some to become sick and others even to die.

In the case of the fellow in 1 Corinthians 5, who was having sexual relations with his father's wife, God threatened to touch his body, and even take his life if he did not repent: *"In the name of our Lord Jesus, when you are assembled, and I with you in spirit, with the power of our Lord Jesus, I have decided to **deliver such a one to Satan for the destruction of his flesh,** so that his spirit may be saved in the day of the Lord Jesus"* (1 Cor. 5:4–5).

We also see how God exercised severe judgment in the life of a woman in Revelation 2:20–23:

> But I have this against you, that you tolerate the woman Jezebel, who calls herself a prophetess, and **she teaches and leads My bond-servants astray so that they commit acts of immorality and eat things sacrificed to idols**. I gave her time to repent, and she does not want to repent of her immorality. Behold, I will **throw her on a bed of sickness, and those who commit adultery with her into great tribulation**, unless they repent of her deeds. And **I will kill her children with pestilence**, and all the churches will know that I am He who searches the minds and hearts; and I will give to each one of you according to your deeds.

Christ took these sins so seriously that He threw Jezebel on a bed of sickness, threw those who committed adultery with her into great tribulation, and killed the children of Jezebel with pestilence.

Church discipline is a way to protect a believer who is living in sin from being judged severely by God. Scripture reveals that God will punish, and even take the life of a believer who is living in sin, if they do not repent.

## 6. It Warns Other Believers to Be Fearful of Sinning

*"Do not receive an accusation against an elder except on the basis of two or three witnesses. Those who continue in sin, rebuke in the presence of all, **so***

*that the rest also will be fearful of sinning"* (1 Tim. 5:19–20).

*"What made you think of doing such a thing? You have not lied to men but to God.' When Ananias heard this, **he fell down and died**. And **great fear seized the whole church** and all who heard about these events"* (Acts 5:4–5).

Church discipline provides a stark and chilling warning to those considering a sinful path. When they see that God uses His church to carry out severe punishment, and even in extreme cases takes the life of a sinful believer, this causes all to pause and take God, and their spiritual purity, seriously.

## 7. It Tests the Obedience Level of a Church and Its Leadership

When the Apostle Paul wrote to the Corinthian church regarding church discipline, one of the reasons he did so was to test their obedience level to God:

*The punishment inflicted on him by the majority is sufficient. Now instead, you ought to forgive and comfort him, so that he will not be overwhelmed by excessive sorrow. I urge you, therefore, to reaffirm your love for him. **Another reason I wrote you was to see if you would stand the test and be obedient in everything** (2 Cor. 2:6–9).*

Church discipline appears to be one of the toughest jobs of church leaders. Therefore, it is a test of their obedience level to God regarding His gift of leadership.

The central and core function of a church is the teaching of God's Word to God's people. If leadership is not willing to obey God in tough matters, then they lose their right to tell the church they should as well. As a result, this core function is sacrificed, and our teaching loses its power and effectiveness.

If people in the church see that leaders don't obey in tough matters, then they will logically conclude that they don't need to either. They subconsciously will learn that some passages apply, and some don't, that some passages are to be obeyed, and some aren't. This is extremely dangerous and erodes the foundation of God's Word, casting us into a sea of confusion and instability.

Picking and choosing what we want to obey in God's Word sets us on the path that has led many godly churches, organizations, and institutes to slowly move away from upholding God's Word to actually promoting messages that are contrary to God's clear teachings.

## Conclusion

One of the great misconceptions in the church today is that corrective church discipline is not needed or is for the sole purpose of restoring a fallen believer living in sin. As we can see, there are at least seven purposes for corrective church discipline:

1. It promotes and protects God's holiness (Ezek. 36:16–21; 1 Cor. 5:1–5).

2. It maintains the standards and faithful witness of Christ's Church to a watching world (Matt. 5:13–16).

3. It protects the purity of the church and keeps sin from spreading throughout its ranks (Josh. 7:3; 1 Cor. 5:6–7).

4. It restores a fellow believer caught in sin and helps them find their way back to God (2 Cor. 2:6–8).

5. It prevents unrepentant believers living in sin from severe judgment (1 Cor. 5:5; 1 Cor. 11:30; Rev. 2:20–23).

6. It warns other believers to be fearful of sinning (1 Tim. 5:19–20).

7. It tests the obedience level of a church and its leadership (2 Cor. 2:9).

Once again, there are more purposes to corrective church discipline than just restoring a believer living in sin. All of these purposes must be taken into consideration if we're going to take Christ and His word seriously.

# Chapter 7

# What Are the Biblical Steps of Corrective Church Discipline?

In Matthew 18:15–20, we find Christ's teaching on corrective church discipline. Matthew 18 provides the structure, and 1 Corinthians 5, and 2 Corinthians 2, deal more with the implementation of it. For the structure, we'll look at the four steps of church discipline found in Matthew 18.

Steps 1–3 deal with doing everything possible to persuade the unrepentant believer to repent and obey God, and step 4 involves placing the unrepentant believer in church discipline if they refuse all that was done in steps 1–3.

### The 4 Steps of the Church Discipline Process

**Step 1:** *"If your brother sins, **go and show him his fault in private**; if he listens to you, you have won your brother"* (Matt. 18:15).

Step 1 involves a one on one private meeting with a believer in sin. What qualifies as a sin that warrants us going to a believer? The answer is that it's not the size of the sin that matters according to Christ, but that a person seems to be sinning either ignorantly in a certain area or sinning on a continual basis with no willingness to repent and stop. This step is not for believers who sin on occasion, repent, and desire to grow and change. It's only for those who are content to stay in their sin with no willingness to repent.

Notice that this first step doesn't say to tell it to

others first, it says for you to go directly to your brother or sister and tell them their sin in private. This doesn't mean, though, that you shouldn't seek some wise counsel from your pastor or a mature believer in Christ beforehand.

Also, you need to be certain that your brother or sister is doing something sinful, not just doing something you don't like, or what you believe is a sin. Please let me explain.

In Scripture, there are liberties that Christians have that are not related to sin. For example, Romans chapter 14 talks about convictions that some believers have or don't have. Some have differences in their convictions about eating certain foods, what day they worship on, or how they might worship. Some might be okay with having a glass of wine or an alcoholic beverage on occasion, while others feel this would be wrong for them.

In these areas of liberties, we need to be certain we're not accusing a believer of something that might be a sin for us but for them is a liberty that is not a sin.

So, when we go to a brother or sister, as commanded in this first step, we need to be certain their sin is a clear violation of a biblical principle that applies to everyone, and not a personal conviction we have that would just apply to us.

**Step 2:** *"But if he does not listen to you, **take one or two more with you**, so that by the mouth of two or three witnesses every fact may be confirmed"* (Matt. 18:16).

Step 2 involves a group meeting including several people. It's important to note that in this step every fact should be confirmed. I believe it's wise at this step to write down and keep track of these facts for future use in case they're needed. Christ talked here about facts, the actions, evidence, or fruit that can document the sin of a believer. We should not entertain feelings, assumptions, gossip, hunches, and so forth from others. Christ tells us we should deal only in cold, hard facts.

This principle of taking one or two witnesses with you in order to establish the facts is found in the Old Testament as well: *"A single witness shall not rise up against a man on account of any iniquity or any sin which he has committed; **on the evidence of two or three witnesses a matter shall be confirmed**"* (Deut. 19:15).

**Sub-step Between Steps 2 and 3:** It appears that between steps 2 and 3 there could be a sub-step that includes bringing the leadership of the church into the process. This seems so as it's the church leadership that should implement and oversee the rest of the church discipline process.

**Step 3:** *"If he refuses to listen to them,* **tell it to the church"** (Matt. 18:17).

Step 3 involves churchwide participation. This could also include many individuals or small groups confronting, counseling, and persuading this unrepentant believer to repent and obey God. In this step, the circle is widened substantially to include the church on a larger scale. The purpose Christ has in mind for this step is that many from the church would personally go to this sinful brother or sister and plead with them to repent and turn to the Lord in obedience. This step could also include a letter from the leadership representing the church, pleading with this sinful person to repent and obey God.

We'll deal extensively with what it means to *"Tell it to the church"* in chapter 8.

**Step 4:** *"And if he refuses to listen even to the church,* **let him be to you as a Gentile and a tax collector"** (Matt. 18:17).

As we'll convincingly learn in chapter 9, this step is a *cutting off, not associating with,* and *expelling from fellowship* a believer who refuses to repent after they have been clearly told by many people over a period of time of their need to get right with the Lord.

## Conclusion

In Matthew 18:15–20, we find Christ's teaching on corrective church discipline. In this passage, we see four clear steps to this process. Steps 1–3 are designed to persuade an unrepentant believer living in sin to repent and return to obedience to Christ. Step 4 is used in cases where an unrepentant believer living in sin refuses to listen and repent of their sin. This last step is what we would define as church discipline.

According to the complete biblical teaching on church discipline, a person who is placed in church discipline is to be expelled from the church, and we are not to associate with them unless it involves some movement on their part seeking to repent and be restored. This might sound harsh, but it is God's loving plan to rescue and restore unrepentant believers and protect the purity of the church.

# Chapter 8

## What Does "Tell It to the Church" Mean?

## What Does, *"Tell It to the Church"* Mean?

There are numerous interpretations of what this means. Biblically speaking, Christ just says, *"If he refuses to listen to them, **tell it to the church**; and if he refuses to listen even to **the church**, let him be to you as a Gentile and a tax collector"* (Matt. 18:17).

The church can be defined in two ways: (1) believers from the whole world who are part of God's Kingdom and family, and (2) a group of believers who make up a local church assembly.

It seems obvious that Christ had in mind the local church assembly when He gave the command, *"Tell it to the church."* After all, it would be logistically impossible for every believer around the whole world to be involved in every case of church discipline.

In the New Testament, we see many examples of local churches who met. Some were huge, like the church in Jerusalem, and some were much smaller, like the house church mentioned in Romans 16:5.

So, the term, *"Tell it to the church"* should simply be interpreted as telling it to the local congregation when they are gathered.

## Do We Tell the Whole Church or Just Part of the Church?

Now, the question that would naturally arise today is that the church has multiple services, the main service taking place on Sunday, and others at different times throughout the week. As a result, should we tell it to just part of the church or the whole church?

Christ does not give details as to whether we should tell the whole church about a church discipline case, just the members of the church (the faithful), or only a small inner circle who knows the person involved in sin.

In order to answer this question, we'll run it through the filter of each of the purposes of church discipline to see which would be the most biblical.

## What Are the Purposes of Church Discipline?

We have already answered this question in chapter 6, but briefly stated, it includes the following purposes: (1) to promote and protect God's holiness (2) to maintain the standards and faithful witness of Christ's Church (3) to protect the purity of the church (4) to restore a brother or sister who is living in unrepentant sin (5) to protect the unrepentant believer living in sin from severe judgment from God (6) to warn other believers in the church about the seriousness of sin, and (7) to test the obedience level of a church and its leadership.

Taking the above purposes into consideration, I would simply ask the question: "What avenue would be best to carry out the purposes of church discipline? By telling it to the whole church, just the faithful attendees, or only a small inner circle who know the situation?"

In order to answer this question, let's take each of the seven purposes of church discipline and run them through the filter of how they would be affected if we told it to the whole church, the members (the faithful), or a small inner circle.

## 1. To Promote and Protect God's Holiness

*"But you are a **chosen race, a royal priesthood, a holy nation**, a people for God's own possession, so that you may proclaim the excellencies of Him who has called you out of darkness into His marvelous light"* (1 Pet. 2:9).

It would seem sensible that as many in the church that could hear this foundational truth would be benefitted as a result. After all, this is a message God upholds throughout Scripture and one we want everyone in our churches to fully grasp. So, for the purpose of promoting and protecting God's holiness, it would be healthy to "tell it to the whole church."

## 2. To Maintain the Standards and Faithful Witness of Christ's Church

*"Let your light shine before men in such a way that they may see your good works and glorify your Father who is in heaven"* (Matt. 5:16).

Surely, we want every member in our church to be a bright shining light for Christ. However, a church that allows sin in its midst becomes a dim light.

We simply don't know how many people in the church, or outside the church, might know about a so-called brother or sister who is living in unrepentant sin. My guess is that more people know than we think. Information like this gets around, especially in smaller towns. For this reason, I would encourage "telling it to the whole church." I think it's better to protect God and the church's reputation than worry about a few people who might not know about the situation and hear about it. Additionally, you have more informed voices that can defend God and the church's reputation to those outside the church who might call those within, hypocrites, for allowing such sin in their midst.

This message is one we would want the whole church to participate in and value. So, for the purpose of maintaining the standards and faithful witness of Christ's Church, it would be healthy to "tell it to the whole church."

## 3. To Protect the Purity of the Church

*"Your boasting is not good. Do you not know that a* **little leaven leavens the whole lump of dough?** *Clean out the old leaven so that you may be a new lump, just as you are in fact unleavened"* (1 Cor. 5:6-7).

I believe we could tell the whole church and we would not damage the purity of anyone. In fact, we would send a powerful message that purity is important. So, to protect the purity of the church, it would be healthy to "tell it to the whole church."

## 4. To Restore a Believer Living in Unrepentant Sin

*"My brothers, if one of you should wander from the truth and someone should bring him back, remember this:* **Whoever turns a sinner from the error of his way will save him from death and cover over a multitude of sins"** (Jam. 5:19–20).

Some might believe it would be best to just tell part of the church so that they could go to an unrepentant believer living in sin and try to restore them. However, it could be argued that those God has in mind to restore this person might not be a part of this group, and as a result, we would be limiting who could be used in this process. Therefore, for the purpose of restoring a believer, it would be healthy to tell the whole church so more voices of persuasion can be involved in trying to win this brother or sister back from their unrepentant state.

If we really believe the wages of sin is death, and that sin really destroys people's lives, then I would see no danger in telling the whole church so that more can be involved in praying and trying to win this unrepentant sinner back to Christ. Therefore, "telling it to the whole church" would be healthy and effective.

## 5. To Protect a Believer Living in Sin From Severe Judgment

*"For this reason, many among you **are weak and sick, and a number sleep** [have died]"* (1 Cor. 11:30).

Church discipline is a way to protect a believer who is living in sin from being judged severely by God. Scripture reveals that God will punish, and even take the life of a believer who is living in sin in some cases. This is a sober message that the whole church should hear. So, to protect a believer living in sin from severe judgment, it would be healthy to "tell it to the whole church."

## 6. To Warn Other Believers in the Church About the Seriousness of Sin

*"Do not receive an accusation against an elder except on the basis of two or three witnesses. Those who continue in sin, **rebuke in the presence of all, so that the rest also will be fearful of sinning"** (1 Tim. 5:19–20).

We clearly see in the case of a church leader who falls into sin that they are to be rebuked in front of the whole church so that everyone else will also be fearful of sinning. If one of the reasons for church discipline is to warn other believers about the seriousness of sin, then "telling it to the whole church" would be healthy and wise as everyone can be warned and become fearful of sinning.

## 7. To Test the Obedience Level of a Church and Its Leadership

*"The punishment inflicted on him by the majority is sufficient. Now instead, you ought to forgive and comfort him, so that he will not be overwhelmed by excessive sorrow. I urge you, therefore, to reaffirm your love for him.* **Another reason I wrote you was to see if you would stand the test and be obedient in everything"** (2 Cor. 2:6–9).

In this purpose for church discipline, God allows the church and its leadership to be on display. How they obey God in this area demonstrates their level of love and obedience to Him. Therefore, I think it would be healthy for the whole church to be a part of displaying their love and obedience to God in exercising church discipline. So, once again, "telling it to the whole church" would be healthy.

## Arguments Against "Telling It to the Whole Church"

One of the main arguments against "telling it to the whole church" is that there might be visitors or unsaved in the church service on a

Sunday. Some feel it would damage them to hear such matters, or that they might gossip about it.

## Response to Arguments Against "Telling It to the Whole Church"

I think we first must define who the church is for and who it includes. The church exists primarily for the edification of believers (Eph. 4), not for the unsaved. Now, while we hope the unsaved attend, the main purpose of the church is not for them.

Therefore, if a matter of church discipline is brought up in a Sunday church service, I don't believe we should fail to carry out an important church issue because we feel we should give priority to a few unsaved people or visitors who might be present.

Also, if we once again understand that a crucial aspect of church discipline is to maintain purity in the church and teach that sin is destructive, then this is not a bad message for the unsaved or visitors to hear. Therefore, I see no negatives in sending a message that a church takes sin seriously and is striving for holiness. This is a wonderful message!

After all, if we believe it's okay to preach a gospel message in the church to the unsaved and visitors where we talk about sin, hell, and other pointed truths that could be considered offensive to them, then why couldn't we deal with church discipline which is the application of these doctrines? Therefore, I see no negative factor as to why the unsaved and visitors would be adversely affected. And if they were, then they probably would not stay at this church very long anyway if other teachings like sin, hell, purity, and so forth are mentioned.

## Two Options in "Telling It to the Church"

**Option 1:** One interpretation of *"Tell it to the church"* (Matt. 18:17) is that Christ was talking about telling it to just the saved Christians in the church. If we choose this interpretation, then the first option would be just to have a meeting with the faithful of the church. We could do this in a special meeting or in a meeting after a regular church service. If we did it after a regular church service, we would then just kindly ask the faithful to stay after church because a family matter is going to be discussed.

**Option 2:** The other interpretation is that in other passages in the New Testament, the church can refer to a group gathered at a local place wherein both believers and non-believers are gathered.

We see this clearly in 1 Corinthians 14, where Paul deals with the gift of tongues in the church:

*Therefore, if the **whole church assembles together** and all speak in tongues, and ungifted men or **unbelievers enter**, will they not say that you are mad? But if all prophesy, **and an unbeliever** or an ungifted man enters, he is convicted by all, he is called to account by all; the secrets of his heart are disclosed; and so, he will fall on his face and worship God, declaring that God is certainly among you* (1 Cor. 14:23–25).

We see in this passage that when the whole church was gathered together there were also unbelievers present as well. This is generally the case in most churches on most Sundays. We also see that these non-believers were convicted of sin as a result of being a part of the church service. This conviction was good and was what led them to repentance. For an unsaved person to witness a church discipline situation, it could be something God uses to bring conviction to their hearts, so it wouldn't be harmful for them to see it.

Using this passage, some would interpret that *"Tell it to the church"* means just that, tell it to the whole church even if non-Christians are present. So, the second option would be to "tell it to the whole church" regardless of who is present.

## Church Discipline Should Not Be Viewed as Negative

It's vital to understand that church discipline should not be viewed as something negative. Instead, when we deal with church discipline, we are sending a loud and strong message that sin is destructive and harmful, and purity is vital for health in the life of a believer and a church. This is about the healthiest message we can promote. It's a message of love that seeks to protect all from the destruction of sin.

Moreover, this is one of the main tasks of leadership. We can preach how bad sin is, but when we exercise church discipline, everyone can see that we mean what we say.

**Conclusion**

When we analyze the seven purposes of church discipline, it appears that there is nothing detrimental about "telling it to the whole church."

Moreover, it appears that *"Tell it to the church"* means just that, tell it to the whole church. I believe this is what Christ had in mind and that there is nothing negative about sending a message that sin is destructive and should be taken seriously. In fact, this is the message the church should be teaching on a regular basis.

# Chapter 9

## What Does It Mean to "Treat Him as a Gentile and a Tax Collector?"

## What Does Christ's Command, "Let Him Be to You as a Gentile and a Tax Collector" Mean?

How we interpret this command is paramount in understanding how to obey Christ in treating an unrepentant believer living in sin, and whether corrective church discipline is part of Christ's command. For this reason, we'll devote this chapter to biblically searching out what Christ meant by this phrase.

There are two basic positions regarding the meaning of this statement:

**1.** Some say that Christ's statement, *"Let him be to you as a Gentile and a tax collector"* means we should treat a disobedient Christian living in unrepentant sin as if they were a non-believer. As a result, it **does not believe in exercising corrective church discipline**, but instead, it believes we should continue a relationship with unrepentant believers like we would with a non-believer. It sees corrective discipline as unloving, judgmental, and harsh. It also does not take into account other New Testament verses that deal with corrective discipline.

**2.** Others say that Christ's statement means we **should exercise corrective church discipline** in the life of a disobedient Christian living in unrepentant sin. This would entail expelling them from the church fellowship and no longer associating with them unless they are seeking restoration. This position takes into account other New Testament verses that deal with corrective discipline.

To be fair, we'll look at both sides of the debate. Following are the two positions and their rationale.

## 1. Arguments in Favor of No Corrective Church Discipline

This position believes that because Jesus interacted with some Gentiles during His ministry, and interfaced with many sinners and tax collectors, that we only need to look at how Christ treated Gentiles and tax collectors to understand what He meant by, *"Let him be to you as a Gentile and a tax collector."*

*And it happened that He was reclining at the table in his house, and **many tax collectors and sinners** were dining with Jesus and His disciples; for there were many of them, and they were following Him. When the scribes of the Pharisees saw that He was eating with the sinners and tax collectors, they said to His disciples, "Why is He eating and drinking with tax collectors and sinners?" And hearing this, Jesus said to them, "It is not those who are healthy who need a physician, but those who are sick; I did not come to call the righteous, but sinners* (Mark 2:15–17).

This position looks at Christ's interaction with the Gentiles, tax collectors, and sinners (of whom all would be non-believers) and believes that *"Let him be to you as a Gentile and tax collector"* means that we should treat believers living in unrepentant sin as unbelievers, and therefore, go to them as if they were a non-Christian, have a relationship with them, eat with them, invite them to church, fellowship with them, and so forth. Once again, this position **does not** believe in corrective church discipline.

## 2. Arguments in Favor of Corrective Church Discipline

This position believes that Christ's statement, *"Let him be to you as a Gentile and a tax collector"* would have been interpreted by the original hearers in the 1st century as a command to implement corrective church discipline. This would entail expelling from the church fellowship an unrepentant believer living in sin and not associating with them.

Additionally, this position takes into consideration other verses in the New Testament that teach the same concept of using corrective church discipline.

I believe this second position to be the most faithful to the texts dealing with how to treat an unrepentant believer living in sin. Therefore, we'll look at the biblical reasons that support this position.

## The Key to Correctly Understanding Christ's Statement

The main reason Christ's statement, *"Let him be to you as a Gentile and a tax collector"* is so misunderstood is because we fail to understand and apply two basic rules of hermeneutics (hermeneutics is the science and art of correct interpretation using rules and laws that apply to all texts and writings).

The first rule of hermeneutics teaches that we must first understand to whom a text is written, and how they would have understood it in their historical context and culture.

The second rule of hermeneutics teaches that we must look at all of what the Bible teaches about a topic or doctrine, not just one verse, or a few selected verses.

Therefore, if we don't follow these basic rules of hermeneutics, we'll miss the true meaning of any topic or doctrine of Scripture.

Taking these important hermeneutical principles into account, the following Bible passages will easily lead us to conclude that the correct interpretation of *"Let him be to you as a Gentile and a tax collector"* means that Christ intended for us to use corrective church discipline in the life of a disobedient Christian living in unrepentant sin.

## A Look at the Context

Christ's command, *"Let him be to you as a Gentile and a tax collector"* is the last of four commands given by Christ regarding how we should confront sin in the life of a sinning brother or sister in Christ:

> *If your brother sins,* **go and show him his fault** *in private; if he listens to you, you have won your brother. But if he does not listen to you,* **take one or two more with you,** *so that by the mouth of two or three witnesses every fact may be confirmed. If he refuses to listen to them,* **tell it to the church;** *and if he refuses to listen even to the church,* **let him be to you as a Gentile and a tax collector** (Matt. 18:15–17).

This last command is the climax of this passage and tells us what to do after all the previous three steps have been followed.

We can't help but notice that each step builds upon the other and becomes more severe in nature. The pressure mounts and the consequences grow. The process starts small and then gets bigger. There's a movement from simple resolution towards a penalty if change is not made.

Therefore, it seems rather anticlimactic that each step would get more severe and then the last step would fizzle away. However, this is what those who don't believe in corrective discipline are forced to embrace. Step 4, according to them, moves the believer out of the pressure into an arena of acceptance. It eliminates corrective discipline and allows them to remain in their state of sin with little or no consequences.

Most parents would not threaten a child with discipline and then let them off the hook if they continued to disobey after being warned repeatedly. However, this is what those who don't believe in corrective discipline seem to uphold by not following through and exercising discipline. They let unrepentant believers off the hook and remove the consequences for their disobedience and rebellion to God. In child-rearing, this philosophy would be a recipe for disaster. It's the same for adults. Therefore, not believing in corrective church discipline does not fit well with the context of this passage and the message it's conveying.

## Who Was Christ Talking To?

When Christ said, *"Let him be to you as a Gentile and a tax collector,"* He was talking to Jews in the 1st century who had an Old Testament worldview. To them, as we will see throughout this chapter, they would have fully understood what He meant. They easily would have interpreted this phrase to mean that they were to have no interaction with a person in corrective discipline and were to cut them off from fellowship (we learned about this in chapter 3).

## Christ Is Speaking About Believers in Sin, Not Non-believers

A key factor to take into consideration in this passage is that Christ is talking about a **brother or sister in Christ** who is involved in some kind of sin. He is not talking about non-believers in sin, **but believers**. This truth is critical to understanding the meaning of this phrase.

How we are commanded to treat believers living in sin and non-believers living in sin are entirely different (we will elaborate on this in chapter 11).

## Christ's Command Is Something Negative

As we have seen, in Matthew 18:15–17, Christ outlines four steps in dealing with an unrepentant believer living in sin. He commands us to follow steps 1–3 before He gives the command, *"Let him be to you as a Gentile and a tax collector."* Whatever this command means, I believe we can all agree it's something negative, not positive, as Christ is referring to the behavior of a hardened, unrepentant believer and how we should deal with them. However, for those who don't believe in church discipline, there is really nothing negative about treating an unrepentant believer like a non-believer. Therefore, not believing in corrective church discipline does not fit the meaning of the text.

## How the Jews Would Have Interpreted Christ's Statement

How would the Jews have understood Christ's statement, *"Let him be to you as a Gentile and a tax collector?"* They would have easily interpreted it as a command to carry out corrective discipline. Why is this so? Because the Jews did not interact with Gentiles or tax collectors in Jesus' day. **They were considered unclean to them**. This is seen in their constant friction with Christ and their charges against Him that He was breaking Old Testament mandates. We can easily see this in the following encounters.

When Jesus entered the house of Levi, the tax-collector, who later became the Apostle Matthew, the Pharisees and scribes began grumbling at His disciples, saying, *"Why do you eat and drink with the tax collectors and sinners?"* (Luke 5:30). The Pharisees would never allow themselves to eat and drink with tax collectors and sinners as Christ did.

Luke tells us the following: *"Now all the tax collectors and the sinners were coming near Him to listen to Him. **Both the Pharisees and the scribes began to grumble, saying, 'This man receives sinners and eats with them'**"* (Luke 15:1–2). The Pharisees and scribes were so convinced that the tax collectors and sinners

*This is why Paul says u dont even eat + sit with them to make the distinction for us*

93

were unclean that they didn't even allow themselves to eat or be in the same place as them.

Zacchaeus, the tax collector, was so eager to listen to Jesus about salvation that he overlooked the ridicule from the Jews and climbed into a sycamore tree so that he might see Jesus when He passed by. Jesus looked at the state of his heart and decided to stop at his home.

When the Jews saw this, they all began to grumble, saying, *"He has gone to be the guest of a man who is a sinner"* (Luke 19:7). On this occasion, not only the Pharisees, but all the Jews were grumbling and judging Jesus for the fact that He went to be a guest of a tax collector, whom they called a sinner. This shows us that the Jews would never have done what Jesus did.

## The Jews Had No Interaction With Gentiles During the Time of Christ

This is clearly seen by a meeting Jesus had with a Samaritan woman:

> *There came a woman of Samaria to draw water. Jesus said to her, "Give Me a drink." For His disciples had gone away into the city to buy food. Therefore, the Samaritan woman said to Him, "How is it that You, being a Jew, ask me for a drink since I am a Samaritan woman?* **For Jews have no dealings with Samaritans** (John. 4:7–9).

The Samaritans were shunned by the Jews and had been cut off from fellowship because they were what the Jews called, "Half-breeds." In other words, the Samaritans were a mixture of part Jewish and Gentile blood. Their ancestors had intermarried with foreign spouses and were, therefore, considered unclean. Thus, the Samaritan woman was shocked when Jesus, a Jew, had any dealings with her.

We can see in these encounters that the Jews would have easily interpreted Christ's statement as a command to carry out corrective discipline in the life of an unrepentant believer. This would entail cutting them off and having no association with them.

## Because Jesus Interacted With Gentiles Doesn't Mean That Is How the Jews Understood Christ's Statement

The fact that Jesus had dealings with Gentiles and sinners shouldn't be used as the example of what Jesus was saying when He said, "*Let him be to you as a Gentile and a tax collector.*"

It's critical to understand to whom Christ was speaking. He said, "Let him (a Gentile and a tax collector) be **to you**," not, "Let him be the way I am treating him." Christ was speaking to the Jewish worldview and their understanding of what this phrase meant, not using Himself as an example of how they should treat Gentiles and sinners. Again, Christ was emphasizing **how the Jews treated**

**Gentiles and tax collectors, not how He treated them**. If we don't understand this clear point, we'll entirely misinterpret this command as many today have done.

## Fear of Being Put Out of the Synagogue

As we saw earlier, a large part of corrective discipline in the Jewish community involved being put out of the synagogue for refusing to repent of sin, not obeying certain laws and practices, and for believing or teaching false doctrine.

To be put out of the synagogue was disastrous for a Jew. It meant they lost their spiritual connection, their social connection, their business connection, their educational connection, their school connection for their children, and on some occasions, their family connection. The church is meant to be our allegion, home, our whole life in christ. Our only allegion the world

Therefore, many of the Jews in Jesus' day did not openly confess Jesus as their Messiah for fear of being put out of the synagogue: *"Nevertheless many even of the rulers believed in Him, but because of the Pharisees they were not confessing Him, **for fear that they would be put out of the synagogue**"* (John 12:42).

The Gentiles, along with Jewish sinners and tax collectors, were all banned from the synagogue and cut-off from the Jewish community. Therefore, when Christ said, *"Let him be to you as a Gentile and a tax collector,"* this would have sent shivers up and down the spines of the Jews. They knew exactly what this entailed; it meant they were to be put out of the synagogue and cut-off from their Jewish community and life like the Gentiles, tax collectors, and sinners were. This was such a severe form of corrective discipline that it was virtually impossible to bear.

## Jesus Was Establishing the New Covenant, So He Did Things Differently Than the Jews

Because Jesus was God, He did many things that the Jews were forbidden to do in the Old Testament (i.e., touch lepers, the dead, the unclean, etc.). This is one of the reasons why the Jews had such a hard time with Jesus.

Sometimes we overlook the fact that Jesus lived and ministered mainly in the Old Covenant Period, and that those He ministered to had an Old Covenant worldview. This is critical in understanding how the Jews would have understood Christ's teaching on the church discipline process and what it entailed.

Therefore, we must understand that Jesus was God and was in the process of establishing the New Covenant. As a result, He did things that the Jews were forbidden to do, but that later, believers were able to do after Christ's death and resurrection, and the New Covenant was given.

The fact that Christ was God and in the process of establishing the New Covenant shouldn't be confused with how the Jews would have clearly understood what the phrase, *"Let him be to you as a Gentile and tax collector"* meant in the Old Covenant.

In the Old Testament Law, Jews were forbidden to fellowship with those who broke God's covenant laws and were even to be "cut off" or stoned to death in some situations (we learned about this in chapter 3 that dealt with how corrective discipline functioned in the Old Testament).

Instead of fellowshipping with unrepentant sinners in the Jewish community, they were commanded to use corrective discipline and "cut them off" and not associate with them. This concept harmonizes with the rest of the New Testament's teaching on how we should treat an unrepentant believer as well.

## Example of Acts 10:28

When the Apostle Peter was sent by the Holy Spirit to take the gospel to the Gentiles, he clearly revealed what it meant not to have any association with Gentiles. Peter said the following, *"And he said to them, 'You yourselves know **how unlawful it is for a man who is a Jew to associate with a foreigner or to visit him;** and yet God has shown me that I should not call any man unholy or unclean.'"*

This verse provides overwhelming clarity as to how the Jews treated Gentiles. It was unlawful for them to associate or visit them, and they were considered unholy and unclean.

We can see in this encounter how the Jews treated the Gentiles and the Samaritans in the 1st century, and how they would have easily interpreted Christ's statement as a command not to have any association with an unrepentant believer living in sin.

## Example of Galatians 2:11–12

*"But when Cephas came to Antioch, I opposed him to his face, because he stood condemned. For prior to the coming of certain men from James, he used to eat with the Gentiles; but when they came, he began to **withdraw and hold himself aloof**, fearing the party of the circumcision."*

Paul rebuked Peter because he withdrew and held himself aloof from Gentile believers due to peer pressure from other Jews. This, once again, reveals that the Jews had no contact with the Gentiles. The only exception to this was for those who joined the Jewish faith.

## How "Let Him Be to You as a Gentile and a Tax Collector" Harmonizes With Other Verses

The following verses harmonize perfectly with what Christ meant by his command, *"Let him be to you as a Gentile and tax collector"* and how the Jews would have understood it. The concept of **no interaction** and **cutting off** is seen clearly in the following passages:

## 1 Corinthians 5:9–13

*"But actually, I wrote to you **not to associate with any so-called brother** if he is an immoral person, or covetous, or an idolater, or a reviler, or a drunkard, or a swindler – **not even to eat with such a one**. What business is it of mine to judge those outside the church? Are you not to judge those inside? God will judge those outside. "**Expel the wicked person from among you**."*

## 2 Thessalonians 3:6

*"Now we command you, brethren, in the name of our Lord Jesus Christ, that you **keep away** from every brother who leads an unruly life and not according to the tradition which you received from us."*

## 2 Thessalonians 3:14

*"Take special note of anyone who does not obey our instruction in this letter. **Do not associate with them**, in order that they may feel ashamed."*

### Treating an Unrepentant Believer as a Non-believer Is Contradictory to Many Verses

Those who believe that the term, "*Let him be to you as a Gentile and a tax collector*" means that we should treat an unrepentant believer as a non-believer hold a belief that is contradictory to other verses.

For example, how do we treat the unsaved? We are commanded to go to them, share Christ with them, build relationships with them, eat with them, and do whatever we can to help them come to Christ. However, we are commanded just the opposite in many other verses that deal with how we are to treat an unrepentant believer.

For instance, on the one hand, according to those who don't believe in corrective discipline, **we are** supposed to treat unrepentant believers like non-Christians and have contact with them, but then, on the other hand, we have many other verses that say **we are not** to have contact with them. Therefore, the interpretation of treating unrepentant believers as non-believers becomes contradictory and conflictive. Moreover, how are we to obey 1 Corinthians 5, and other similar verses where we have clear commands on how we should treat unrepentant believers living in sin?

*"I wrote you in my letter* **not to associate** *with immoral people;* **I did not at all mean with the immoral people of this world***, or with the covetous and swindlers, or with idolaters, for then you would have to go out of the world. But actually, I wrote to you* **not to associate with any so-called brother** *if he is an immoral person, or covetous, or an idolater, or a reviler, or a drunkard, or a swindler – not even to eat with such a one"* (1 Cor. 5:9–11).

When Paul says: *"***I did not at all mean with the immoral people of this world***,"* he is clearly drawing a distinction between how we treat believers in sin and the unsaved. We are commanded **not** to have contact with unrepentant believers, but we **are** commanded to have contact with the unsaved of the world. *only with the intent to win them like Jesus did*

Additionally, Paul commands us to expel a believer living in unrepentant sin: "*What business is it of mine to judge those outside the church? Are you not to judge those inside? God will judge those outside.* "**Expel the wicked person from among you**" (1 Cor. 5:12–13).

We certainly are not to expel non-believers from our churches. Just the contrary, we are to do all we can to get them to church.

Therefore, treating an unrepentant believer like an unsaved person conflicts with many passages. To me, it's forcing Scripture to mean what I want it to say instead of just letting God's Word speak for itself.

## Church Discipline Is Considered a Form of Punishment

Church discipline is a form of corrective discipline and entails some sort of punishment. When Paul wrote to the Corinthian Church in 2 Corinthians, he spoke about receiving back into the fellowship the brother who had been put in church discipline in 1 Corinthians 5: "*The **punishment inflicted on him by the majority is sufficient.** Now instead, you ought to forgive and comfort him, so that he will not be overwhelmed by excessive sorrow. I urge you, therefore, to reaffirm your love for him*" (2 Cor. 2:6–8).

Here we see that the Apostle Paul referred to corrective church discipline as a form of punishment. This would be something we would never do to a non-believer. Moreover, nowhere in Scripture is the church commanded to punish non-believers because of their sins. Therefore, this passage contradicts the belief that we are to treat unrepentant believers like non-believers and not exercise corrective discipline.

## What About the Other Commands of Christ in the Corrective Discipline Process?

For those who don't believe in utilizing corrective discipline because it believes we are to treat unrepentant believers like non-believers, what do they do with the other commands in Matthew 18:15–17, that outline the process for corrective discipline?

Do they go to a sinning brother or sister to confront them, do they take two or three others with them if this sinning believer refuses to listen, and do they tell it to the church if they refuse to listen to the group of two or three?

The answer is that maybe they fulfill steps 1 and 2 of the corrective discipline process, but they certainly don't fulfill step 3, and *"Tell it to the church."* Therefore, they still fall short of obedience to Christ and His commands in this area.

I have yet to hear a sound argument from any who don't believe in corrective discipline as to how they can justify avoiding the clear command to *"Tell it to the church"* regarding the sin of an unrepentant believer in their midst. This is a blatantly clear command that is hard to get around.

## Conclusion

Of the two positions on the meaning of Christ's command, *"Let him be to you as a Gentile and a tax collector,"* we have seen from the overwhelming evidence of Scripture that it **does not** support treating an unrepentant believer like an unsaved person, and as a result, not exercising corrective church discipline. We just have too many verses that say the contrary.

We also can clearly see that corrective church discipline is found all throughout Scripture and is, therefore, a biblical concept.

Additionally, those who do not believe in corrective church discipline have failed to apply two basic rules of hermeneutics. The first rule teaches that we must first understand to whom a text is written, and how they would have understood it in their historical context and culture, and the second rule teaches that we must look at all of what the Bible teaches about a topic or doctrine, not just one verse, or a few selected verses. If we don't follow these basic rules, then we'll miss the true meaning of any topic or doctrine in Scripture. Therefore, the failure of using these basic rules is the reason many don't believe in church discipline.

Moreover, to the Jewish mind, *"Let him be to you as a Gentile and a tax collector,"* would have easily been interpreted as a command to exercise corrective church discipline in the life of an unrepentant believer living in sin. The rest of the New Testament supports this same concept as well, and as a result, we have a harmonious connection between them and Christ's statement.

Therefore, we can biblically conclude that the true meaning of *"Let him be to you as a Gentile and tax collector,"* is a command given by Christ to exercise corrective church discipline in the life of an unrepentant believer living in sin.

# Chapter 10

## Who Should Be Put in Church Discipline?

## What Kinds of Sin Qualify for Church Discipline?

What qualifies as a sin that warrants putting a believer in church discipline? In step 1 of the church discipline process, Christ says the following: *"If your brother sins, go and **show him his fault in private**; if he listens to you, you have won your brother"* (Matt. 18:15).

The answer to this question is that it's not the size of the sin that matters according to Christ, but that a person seems to be sinning in a certain area on a change continual basis and refuses to listen and repent. In other words, it's for a believer who chooses to **live in sin willfully**. Church discipline is **not** for those who sin on occasion, repent, and desire to grow and change. It's only for those who **refuse to listen** to those who are warning them about their sin.

This is clearly understood by the rest of the verses Christ used regarding the process of church discipline: *"But if he **does not listen to you**, take one or two more with you, so that by the mouth of two or three witnesses every fact may be confirmed. If he **refuses to listen** to them, tell it to the church; and if he **refuses to listen** even to the church, let him be to you as a Gentile and a tax collector"* (Matt. 18:16–17).

We can see in these verses that it's a believer who is living in sin and refuses to listen to everyone who goes to them throughout steps 1–3 of the church discipline process that qualifies for church discipline. Once again, it's not the size of the sin that matters to Christ, but the fact that a person chooses to live in unrepentant sin. Therefore, church discipline is for a believer who is involved in sin on a continual basis and refuses to repent and be restored.

## Biblical Uses of Corrective Church Discipline

We tend to believe that church discipline is only for serious sexual sins, divorce, severe abuses, and so forth. However, Scripture outlines other reasons for church discipline as well.

1. It's for believers living in any unrepentant sin (Matt. 18:15–20; 1 Cor. 5).

2. It's for troublemakers and those who sow discord (Rom. 16:17).

3. It's for the unruly and disorderly (1 Thess. 5:14).

4. It's for drunkards, or also in today's culture, drug addicts (1 Cor. 5:11).

5. It's for swindlers who deceive and steal (1 Cor. 5:11).

6. It's for revilers. To revile is to criticize in an abusive or hostile way, or to spread negative information (1 Cor. 5:11).

7. It's for extreme covetousness, greed, and acquisitive grasping for materialism and other's possessions (1 Cor. 5:11).

8. It's for those who disobey or deny the foundational doctrines of the faith (2 Thess. 3:13–14).

9. It's for those who teach false doctrine regarding the essential aspects of the faith (Rev. 2:14–16)

## Conclusion

According to Christ, it's not the size of the sin that matters in the church discipline process, but that a believer seems to be sinning in a certain area on a continual basis with no willingness to repent and be restored. It is **not** for those who sin on occasion, repent, and desire to grow and change, but is only for those who **refuse to listen** after being warned repeatedly about their sin.

# Chapter 11

## How Should We Treat Christians in Church Discipline?

Although we've already learned a great deal about how we should treat an unrepentant believer in corrective church discipline, in this chapter, we'll look at this essential aspect from several different angles and glean more insight as a result. It's vital we thoroughly understand how to treat a believer in church discipline, so we know how to love them best and follow God's wisdom in this area.

So, how should we treat a believer living in unrepentant sin who is placed in church discipline? What kind of contact should the body of Christ have with this person? This is a debated topic among leading scholars and pastors today.

How we understand God's will in this matter will depend on three key factors: (1) how we understand corrective discipline in the Old Testament (2) how we understand Christ's command, "*Let him be to you as a Gentile and tax collector,*" and (3) how we understand the rest of the New Testament verses dealing with church discipline.

Following are the three main positions on how to treat a believer in church discipline. Later in this chapter, we'll analyze each position to see which is the most biblical.

## Three Main Positions on How to Treat Unrepentant Believers

**Position 1:** This position believes that nothing should change in our relationship with an unrepentant believer living in sin, and we are just to accept them, pray for them, and not be judgmental regarding their sinful activity. Therefore, this position rejects corrective church discipline and **does not** believe in using it.

*no*

**Position 2:** This position believes that we are to treat unrepentant believers as non-believers and do all we can to develop a relationship with them, encourage them, counsel them, and so forth. This position also largely rejects corrective church discipline and **does not** believe in exercising it.

*already been done*

Some in this position do, however, acknowledge some form of church discipline, but it is conflictive in nature. For example, they believe church discipline entails treating unrepentant believers living in sin as non-believers, and that we should develop a relationship with them, encourage them, counsel them, fellowship with them, and so forth. However, this kind of treatment entails no consequences for their sin and refusal to repent. Therefore, their version of church discipline really amounts to no discipline at all.

**Position 3:** This position believes in exercising corrective church discipline. It believes we should do this by cooperating with God in applying supernatural pressure to those in church discipline to repent. It believes they have been told repeatedly what they need to do, and therefore, don't need more knowledge as to what to do, but need to simply decide to return to God and obey Him. In order to cooperate with God, they believe that church discipline entails expelling the unrepentant believer from the church fellowship and not associating with them unless it involves some movement on their part seeking to repent and be restored.

## Which Position Is Biblically Correct?

Because our passion in this book is to let God say what He says, let's look at His Word to hear His position on the matter. We'll first deal with how we should treat an unrepentant believer living in sin according to Jesus, and then we'll look at what the rest of the New Testament says. When we're done, I believe it will be very clear what God's will is in this matter.

## How to Treat a Believer in Corrective Church Discipline According to Jesus

Jesus gives us four steps to follow when attempting to restore a fellow believer who is caught in sin. However, after all these steps have been utilized and we come to step 4, how do we treat an unrepentant believer who has rejected everything and chooses to live in their sin?

114

In order to answer this question, we'll briefly look again at the four steps of the church discipline process Christ outlines in Matthew 18:15–17. As we will see, the way we treat a believer in the corrective discipline process in steps 1–3 is entirely different than step 4. Many are confused about this, so we'll delve into God's Word to fully understand this vital truth.

Jesus outlines four steps to follow:

1. Go and show your brother his fault in private, seeking restoration (Matt. 18:15).

2. If this person does not respond to your private admonition, involve one or two other trusted, mature Christians so that every fact may be confirmed (Matt. 18:16).

3. If this person still will not listen, bring the matter to the church leaders so they can tell it to the church. In so doing, the faithful from the church can go to this person and try to convince them to turn from their sin.

Unfortunately, when a believer refuses all the persuasion carried out in steps 1–3, then they enter step 4.

4. Because this person has rejected and refused to listen to the church, then they are to be treated as a **Gentile and a tax collector.**

According to Jesus (as we learned in chapter 9), this command means we are to exercise corrective discipline and expel unrepentant believers from the church fellowship and not associate with them unless it involves some movement on their part seeking to repent and be restored.

## Does Jesus Want Us to Continue Utilizing Steps 1–3 in Step 4 of the Church Discipline Process?

I don't think so. I see step 4 as distinct from steps 1–3. Steps 1–3 involve showing the person their sin, persuading them to repent, and pleading with them to choose God's will instead of their own. However, when they refuse to listen, then step 4 uses a totally different way of dealing with them. It is a *cutting off, no association*, and *expelling from fellowship* method as seen in Scripture (Matt. 18:17; 1 Cor. 5). So, I believe that step 4 is designed to increase the pressure on the unrepentant believer to repent and is, therefore, God's way of dealing with them differently than what was used in steps 1–3.

In step 4, they are in the hands of God in a unique way and will experience His hand of discipline in their lives. Additionally, the church will be cooperating with God in expelling them from fellowship and not associating with them

(Matt. 18:17; 1 Cor. 5). This will speak volumes and show them the severity of their sin. They have already heard everything they need to know countless times in steps 1–3, so they don't need more knowledge and persuasion; they need pressure to obey what they know they should do.

The whole reason for step 4 is to apply more pressure. The loss of their relationship with the church and their relationship with God's people, plus God supernaturally working in their heart and life, is what applies greater pressure for them to obey. For this reason, I don't believe we should continue to utilize steps 1–3 in the church discipline process, and there should be no association with them unless it involves the believer in church discipline making contact showing their desire to repent and return to God.

When they do repent, believers and the church should rush in to restore them, welcome them back, and shower them with relational love and fellowship.

The attitude of believers and the church during this time of church discipline is like that of the father of the prodigal son. We pray for them, we wait for them, and we look for them. The moment they return, then we welcome them back, kill the fatted calf, and rejoice that a brother lost has returned.

## The Uniqueness of Step 4

Step 4 brings in the supernatural hand of God wherein He takes into consideration the church's actions of "binding and loosing" concerning an unrepentant believer in church discipline. This is seen in Christ's teaching in Matthew 18 that deals with the church discipline process: *"Truly I tell you, whatever you **bind on earth will be bound in heaven, and whatever you loose on earth will be loosed in heaven.** Again, truly I tell you that if **two of you on earth agree about anything they ask for, it will be done for them by my Father in heaven.** For where two or three gather in my name, there am I with them"* (Matt. 18:18–20).

This act of binding and loosing can be quite severe as seen in the corrective discipline case in 1 Corinthians 5: *"In the name of our Lord Jesus, when you are assembled, and I with you in spirit, with the power of our Lord Jesus, I have decided to **deliver such a one to Satan for the destruction of his flesh**, so that his spirit may be saved in the day of the Lord Jesus"* (1 Cor. 5:4–5). It is possible that God will allow Satan to inflict physical punishment, or even take the life of the believer in church discipline if they refuse to repent.

Psalm 32 also speaks about what God does supernaturally in the heart and life of a believer in church discipline: *"When I kept silent about my sin, **my body wasted away through my groaning all day long.** For **day and night, Your hand was heavy upon me; my** *vitality was drained away as with the fever heat of summer"* (Ps. 32:3–4). This verse is King David's account of how God dealt with him when he did not repent of his sin of adultery with Bathsheba, and of murdering her husband, Uriah.

## Summary of How We Should Treat a Believer in Church Discipline According to Jesus

According to Jesus, His command to *"Let him be to you as a Gentile and tax collector"* means we are to exercise church discipline and expel an unrepentant believer from the church fellowship and not associate with them unless it involves some movement on their part seeking to repent and be restored.

Additionally, we should not continue utilizing steps 1–3 of the corrective discipline process in step 4. Step 4 is distinct from steps 1–3. Steps 1–3 involve showing the person their sin, persuading them to repent, and pleading with them to choose God's will instead of their own. However, when they refuse to listen, then step 4 uses a totally different way of dealing with them. It is a ***cutting off, no association***, and ***expelling from fellowship*** method as seen in Scripture (Matt. 18:17; 1 Cor. 5).

## How to Treat an Unrepentant Believer According to the Rest of the New Testament

Now let's look at how God directs us to treat an unrepentant believer living in sin in the rest of the New Testament.

1. *"But now I am writing to you that **you must not associate** with anyone who claims to be a brother or sister but is sexually immoral or greedy, an idolater or slanderer, a drunkard or swindler. **Do not even eat with such people.** What business is it of mine to judge those outside the church? Are you not to judge those inside? God will judge those outside. **Expel the wicked person from among you**"* (1 Cor. 5:11–13).

2. *"In the name of the Lord Jesus Christ, we command you, brothers, to **keep away** from every brother who is idle and does not live according to the teaching you received from us"* (2 Thess. 3:6).

3. *"If anyone does not obey our instruction in this letter, take special note of him. **Do not associate with him, in order that he may feel ashamed.** Yet do not regard him as an enemy, but warn him as a brother"* (2 Thess. 3:14–15).

4. *"Warn a divisive person once, and then warn him a second time. After that, **have nothing to do with him.** You may be sure that such a man is warped and sinful; he is self-condemned"* (Tit. 3:10–11).

5. *"I urge you, brothers, to watch out for those who cause divisions and put obstacles in your way that are contrary to the teaching you have learned. **Keep away**"*

*from them. For such people are not serving our Lord Christ, but their own appetites. By smooth talk and flattery, they deceive the minds of naive people"* (Rom. 16:17–18).

## Summary of How We Should Treat an Unrepentant Believer According to the Rest of the New Testament

These verses we've just looked at tell us that we are to expel from the church fellowship believers in church discipline, not associate with them, not eat with them, to keep away from them, and have nothing to do with them.

When we combine these verses with the Old Testament concept of corrective discipline, and Christ's command, *"Let him be to you as a Gentile and tax collector,"* we can see the clear biblical teaching on this topic.

## Which of the Three Positions on How to Treat an Unrepentant Believer Is the Most Biblical?

At the beginning of this chapter, we mentioned we would analyze each position to see which one is the most biblical. Following are the three positions with a summary of whether they harmonize with God's Word or not.

**Position 1:** This position believes that nothing should change in our relationship with an unrepentant believer living in sin, and we are just to accept them, pray for them, and not be judgmental regarding their sinful activities. Therefore, this position rejects and **does not** believe in corrective church discipline.

**Response:** While this is a popular position embraced by many Christians today, it eliminates corrective church discipline. In so doing, it contradicts the Old Testament concept of corrective discipline, how the Jews would have understood Christ's command, *"Let him be to you as a Gentile and tax collector,"* and the rest of the New Testament verses on how we treat an unrepentant believer living in sin.

For example, we are commanded not to associate with an unrepentant believer living in sin (1 Cor. 5:9), not to eat with them (1 Cor. 5:11), to expel them from the church fellowship (1 Cor. 5:12–13), to consider them as under punishment (2 Corinthians 2:6), to allow them to feel ashamed (2 Thess. 3:14), to keep away from them (2 Thess. 3:6), and so forth.

Because this position contradicts what God teaches us throughout the entire Bible concerning how we should treat an unrepentant believer living in sin, it is not a biblical position and must, therefore, be rejected.

**Position 2:** This position believes that we are to treat unrepentant believers as non-believers and do all we can to develop a relationship with them, share Christ with them, encourage them, fellowship with them, and counsel them. This position also **does not** believe in corrective church discipline.

**Response:** Similar to position 1, this position does not believe in corrective church discipline which makes it virtually impossible to reconcile with the Old Testament concept of corrective discipline, what Jesus taught, and the rest of the New Testament teaching on this issue.

It would also make no sense, according to this position, that we should treat unrepentant believers as non-believers because it wouldn't be a truthful act or command. Unrepentant believers are just that, believers. They are **not non-believers.** So, to treat them as a non-believer would not be a truthful act or command given by Christ.

Moreover, according to this position, we **can and should** associate with an unrepentant believer living in sin, eat with them, fellowship with them, encourage them to attend church, and not view them as under discipline, all of which is contrary to clear commands we have telling us to do the exact opposite.

Therefore, like Position 1, Position 2 does not believe in using corrective church discipline, which contradicts what God teaches us throughout the entire Bible about how we should treat an unrepentant believer living in sin. As a result, it is not a biblical position and must be rejected as well.

**Position 3:** This position believes that we should cooperate with God in supernaturally working in the life of a believer by using corrective church discipline. This means we should expel them from the church fellowship and not associate with them unless it involves some movement on their part seeking to repent and be restored.

**Response:** This position is the most biblical as it believes in corrective church discipline, which harmonizes best with the Old Testament, Christ's teaching, and the rest of the New Testament concerning how we treat an unrepentant believer living in sin.

## Tough Love

Expelling and not associating with a believer in church discipline is designed to cooperate with God in causing them to repent and be restored. It's tough love which is, unfortunately, the last resort in the life of a believer living in sin.

Unfortunately, as we have seen, many Christians today do not believe in corrective church discipline. Instead, they believe in a misapplied version of love that only promotes accepting, encouraging, fellowshipping, and praying for believers living in unrepentant sin.

Now, while we are commanded to love and pray for our Christian brothers and sisters living in unrepentant sin, what do we do when they refuse to change? In their case, God commands us to exercise a different kind of love. It's a form of love that is disciplinary, a kind of love that seeks to save and redeem.

It's called corrective church discipline and is designed by God to rescue a hardened, unrepentant Christian from their sinful choices so that they don't destroy their lives, damage the testimony of the church, bring reproach to Christ, and fall into greater judgment from God. It's a form of discipline for the purpose of restoration and protection.

Wayne Mack states: "Though it may seem a completely unloving thing to put someone out of the fellowship of the church, Jesus commanded us to do this when someone refuses to repent of his or her sin. In reality, since Jesus commanded it, it would be unloving not to do it.[18]

---

[18] Wayne Mack, *To Be or Not To Be a Church Member*, Calvary Press, www.calvarypress.com, 2004, p. 70.

## Conclusion

According to Christ and the other New Testament authors, corrective church discipline is biblical and should be used in the life of an unrepentant believer living in sin. As a result, our relationship with them should change. We should not associate with them (1 Cor. 5:9), we should not eat with them (1 Cor. 5:11), they are to be expelled from the church fellowship (1 Cor. 5:12–13), we should consider them as under punishment (2 Cor. 2:6), they are to feel shame (2 Thess. 3:14), we are to keep away from them (2 Thess. 3:6), and so forth. This sounds harsh, but it's the biblical commands we are given.

The only exception to having contact with a believer in church discipline would be if it involves some movement on their part seeking to repent and be restored.

It's always important to understand when we see biblical truths that seem harsh to us that it's not our role to replace God's wisdom with ours. If we do, we place ourselves above God and make Him subservient to us. This is blasphemy and reckless, but unfortunately, a regular occurrence in much of modern-day Christianity. *idolatry, unbelief, sin*

For those who call themselves believers yet are living in sin with no willingness to change, the church, and every Christian should follow God's will in exercising loving church discipline in their lives. This is God's remedy for rescuing hardened Christians who are living in unrepentant sin. It's a form of "intensive care" discipleship to be used for saving a sick believer who is in the grips of spiritual death.

# Chapter 12

## How to Treat
## Non-Christians in Sin

## Are We Confused?

Many pastors and Christians seem confused regarding the difference between how God commands us to treat non-believers living in sin (which is always the case because they are unsaved) and believers living in sin. They lump both categories together and treat them the same. They fail to understand that God makes a clear distinction in Scripture between non-Christians and Christians, and has clear distinctions regarding His expectations of them.

For the non-Christian living in sin, God commands us to love and welcome them with open arms into our lives and churches. With sincere hearts, we should be open to ministering to sinners just like Christ did. He was called, *"A friend of sinners"* (Luke 7:34), and we should be too. However, we should not be friends with sinners to support them in their sin, but instead, we are to share Christ's Word with them and do everything possible to convince them to embrace Christ as their Savior and turn away from their sins.

God commands us to love all people, but He does not command us to love their sinful activities. In fact, He says just the opposite. The good news is that all sins can be forgiven through Christ's death on the Cross. However, these activities are still sinful. To tell people practicing sinful activities that their sin is okay is not love, but misleading. If we mislead them into believing a lie, then we'll give an account to God for doing so. Therefore, we are to love sinners and share Christ with them, but not endorse, celebrate, or support them in their sin.

## Why Do We Treat Unrepentant Christians in Sin Differently Than Non-Christians in Sin?

We treat them very differently because unlike a non-Christian, the Christian is born-again, knows God, has His Spirit and power within them enabling them to do right, has God's Word that instructs them against sin, and has the church and believers guiding and helping them.

The non-Christian is dead in their trespasses and sins and unable to change without Christ's help. The Christian is alive in Christ and is blessed with all spiritual blessings in heavenly places (Eph. 1:3). Believers, therefore, have no excuse for falling into continual sin.

## Conclusion

We are to fulfill the Great Commission by going to all non-Christians, building relationships with them, and sharing the gospel with them.

For the non-Christian living in sin, God commands us to love and welcome them with open arms into our lives and churches. With sincere hearts, we should be open to ministering to sinners just like Christ did. He was called, *"A friend of sinners"* (Luke 7:34), and we should be too.

However, how we treat non-believers living in sin and how we treat believers living in sin is entirely different. Failing to understand the difference leads to failure in following God's will for each category of people.

# Chapter 13

# What Does God Do When a Church Puts a Sinful Believer in Church Discipline?

## God Is in Our Midst

When referring to church discipline in Matthew 18, Jesus says, *"Truly I say to you, whatever you **bind on earth shall have been bound in heaven; and whatever you loose on earth shall have been loosed in heaven.** Again, I say to you, that **if two of you agree on earth about anything that they may ask, it shall be done for them** by My Father who is in heaven. **For where two or three have gathered together in My name, I am there in their midst**"* (Matt. 18:18–20).

This passage reveals what God does when a church puts a sinful, unrepentant person in church discipline. It's a very misquoted passage many use to say that God is in their midst when two or three gather together for some meeting. Now, while this is true, the context of these verses is dealing with church discipline and what God does when two or three agree about something concerning it.

## It Releases the Hand of God in a Unique Way

Church discipline releases the hand of God to work in an unrepentant believer's life in a unique way. They will now see that all the troubles and problems they are facing (of which many will come supernaturally by God) are not circumstances but are directly from God who is disciplining them and pressuring them to turn from their sinful choices. It brings God into the picture in a clear manner. It is no longer just people urging them to repent, but now God is pressuring them as well.

## How God Moves

Following are some ways God moves when a church prayerfully puts an unrepentant believer in church discipline:

1. **God deals personally with the unrepentant sinner's soul and spirit.**

   *"For day and night **Your hand was heavy upon me;** my vitality was drained away as with the fever heat of summer"* (Ps. 32:4). This verse is King David's account of how God dealt with him when he did not repent of his sin of adultery with Bathsheba, and of murdering her husband, Uriah.

2. **God deals personally with the unrepentant sinner's body, and in some cases, takes their life.**

   God often afflicts them with health problems, or in severe cases, will take their life. *"When I kept silent about my sin, **my body wasted away** through my groaning all day long"* (Ps. 32:3). Once again, this verse is King David's account of how God dealt with him when he did not repent of his sins.

   *"In the name of our Lord Jesus, when you are assembled, and I with you in spirit, with the power of our Lord Jesus, I have decided to deliver such a one to Satan for the **destruction of his flesh,** so that his spirit may be saved in the day of the Lord Jesus"* (1 Cor. 5:4–5). In this

account of church discipline exercised by Paul in the Corinthian Church, the unrepentant believer was handed over to Satan for the destruction of his flesh.

*"But a man must examine himself, and in so doing he is to eat of the bread and drink of the cup. For he who eats and drinks, eats and drinks judgment to himself if he does not judge the body rightly.* **For this reason, many among you are weak and sick, and a number sleep [have died]"** (1 Cor. 11:28–30). Some in the Corinthian Church were living in sin but taking communion like everything was okay. In some cases, God caused sickness and death as a result.

The following passage reveals how Christ gave a woman, Jezebel, time to repent, but after she refused to do so, He stepped in:

*"But I have this against you, that you tolerate the woman Jezebel, who calls herself a prophetess, and she teaches and leads My bond-servants astray so that they commit acts of immorality and eat things sacrificed to idols.* **I gave her time to repent,** *and she does not want to repent of her immorality. Behold, I will* **throw her on a bed of sickness, and those who commit adultery with her into great tribulation,** *unless they repent of her deeds. And* **I will kill her children with pestilence,** *and all the churches will know that I am He who searches the minds and hearts; and I will give to each one of you according to your deeds"* (Rev. 2:20–23).

Christ took these sins so seriously that He threw Jezebel on a bed of sickness, threw those who committed adultery with her into great tribulation, and killed the children of Jezebel with pestilence.

Christ gave Jezebel time to repent, but she refused to do so. I believe God often will do the same in an unrepentant believer's life today. God will grant grace and give them time to repent, but at some point, He might also step in and act severely in their life. This is a sober warning for us all!

3. **God brings unique circumstances and problems into the unrepentant sinner's life.**

   *"Good understanding gains favor, but the way of the unfaithful is hard"* (Prov. 13:15). God will supernaturally do things in a believer's life who is in church discipline, so they'll know what they are experiencing is from Him.

## Warning an Unrepentant Believer About the Consequences of Their Sin

In virtually every circumstance where a believer is living in unrepentant sin, they are blind to the consequences of their choices. They magnify what they believe are the blessings of their sin and diminish the reality of the long-term consequences. So, the truth is, they are short-sighted. What they need is sight to see the long-term consequences of their sin.

When Nathan the prophet went to confront King David about his sin with Bathsheba, and of murdering Uriah, Bathsheba's husband, he revealed to David how much God had blessed him and the consequences he would receive as a response to his sins.

I believe we find here a biblical example of how to confront believers living in unrepentant sin. We should remind them of all God's blessings He has given them, and then help them see clearly the short, and long-term consequences their sinful choices will bring them.

Following are some examples of the consequences we could use to help unrepentant believers living in sin understand the ramifications of their choices:

1. You will damage your relationship with Christ.

2. You will grieve the heart of God.

3. You will damage the testimony of Christ.

4. You will damage the testimony of the Church.

5. You will damage your own testimony.

6. You will give up your moral authority to speak into the lives of others (what right will you have to say to others that they should obey God if you are unwilling to?).

7. You will give up your ability to fulfill the Great Commission because you will unlikely share Christ with others because of your sin and hypocrisy.

8. You will introduce destructive seeds into your family lineage. *spouse + children*

9. You will lose the respect of others.

10. You will lose the respect of your family.

11. You will grieve the heart of your parents.

12. You will stunt or remove the possibility of being transformed into the image of Christ and of reaching spiritual maturity. *No OSHAS*

13. You will lose many eternal rewards. *you will die*

14. You will lose a deep sense of joy from the Lord that comes as we suffer and obey Him in difficult times.

15. You will lose your ministry and service to Christ.

16. You will likely be excluded in the future from eldership or key leadership positions in ministry.

17. You will incur church discipline wherein you will experience God's heavy hand upon you, and in some cases, God might even take your life.

## Conclusion

When a church places a believer living in unrepentant sin in church discipline, it releases the hand of God to work in their life in a unique way. In fact, I believe God sits on the edge of His chair waiting for churches to act so that He can work in a unique way, not only in the person's life in church discipline, but in the lives of those in the church as well.

Sometimes putting an unrepentant believer living in sin seems severe, but we always need to remind ourselves of the consequences of not dealing with sin in our church. John MacArthur provides rich insight:

> Discipline sometimes must be severe because the consequences of not disciplining are much worse. Sin is a spiritual malignancy, and it will not long stay isolated. Unless removed it will spread its infection until the whole fellowship of believers is diseased.[19]

When a church does not place a believer living in unrepentant sin in church discipline, God can still work, but His work is not as visible to the sinful believer and to the rest of the church.

God wants the church to cooperate with Him in rescuing a believer living in unrepentant sin and see them restored in their relationship to Him and the church fellowship. If we truly love believers who have fallen into sin, and if we truly believe that sin brings death and destruction, then we will cooperate with God in exercising church discipline so we can rescue and restore fallen believers.

When sin is left undealt with, it spreads like cancer in the church and hardens those living in sin to continue in disobedience. Therefore, there is nothing positive about not exercising church discipline.

---

[19] John MacArthur, *1 Corinthians*, Moody, 1984, p. 127.

# Chapter 14

## Why Is There Very Little Church Discipline Today?

## Leadership Fails to Understand That Purity in the Church Is One of Their Main Responsibilities

Leadership in the church has several main functions: (1) to teach sound doctrine (2) protect the flock against false doctrine, and (3) to promote purity, holiness, and complete obedience to God in all matters (Matt. 28:20).

In the book of Revelation, these factors were the key issues Christ dealt with in the seven churches (Rev. chapters 2–3).

Hebrews 13:7, also speaks of the importance of the church to imitate the lives of those in leadership: *"Remember those who led you, who spoke the word of God to you; and **considering the result of their conduct, imitate their faith**."* How tragic for the church to imitate leaders who fail to obey God's Word in implementing church discipline when needed.

Additionally, leaders are supposed to watch over the state of purity and obedience in the church: *"Obey your leaders and submit to them, for they keep watch over your souls as those who will give an account. Let them do this with joy and not with grief, for this would be unprofitable for you"* (Heb. 13:17).

Leaders are to keep watch over the souls of those in their churches and will give an account to God for this. How tragic when leaders fail to realize their God-given role and allow believers to live in unrepentant sin without implementing corrective church discipline.

## The Fear of What Others Will Think

*"The **fear of man** brings a snare, but he who trusts in the Lord will be exalted"* (Prov. 29:25). When we face the giants in our lives, which are the tough decisions and choices we must make, we basically have two options: we can choose to fear man, which is a snare, or we can fear God and be exalted. Which choice do you think is the most profitable? However, which option do we choose much of the time?

I love the story of the Prophet Micaiah in the Bible. He is the perfect example of a person who chose to fear God instead of man (1 Kings 22). His situation, however, was much more severe than most of us will ever face.

The Prophet Micaiah lived and prophesied during the time after the nation of Israel had been divided. Ahab was a wicked king over Israel (northern part of Israel), and Jehoshaphat was a righteous king over Judah (southern part of Israel). Ahab wanted to retake a town that had fallen into the possession of the King of Assyria. Ahab asked Jehoshaphat to go with him in battle to retake this city. Because Jehoshaphat was a good king who feared the Lord, he asked Ahab if there was a prophet in the land who could tell them what the Lord's will was in this matter.

Ahab gathered 400 of the key prophets which represented the maximum spiritual voice in the land. All these prophets said to go and take the city. However, Jehoshaphat still had his doubts and asked Ahab if there wasn't one more prophet in the land who could speak to this issue. Ahab said, *"There is yet one man by whom we may inquire of the Lord, but I hate him, because he does not prophesy good concerning me, but evil. He is Micaiah son of Imlah"* (1 Kings 22:8). Then, Jehoshaphat asked that Micaiah be brought before them to speak about what God's will was for them.

Now let's consider what the Prophet Micaiah was facing when he chose whether he would fear man or God. Scripture says that King Ahab and King Jehoshaphat were both arrayed in their royal garments on their thrones. They did this to show their power and authority. Additionally, there were all the big-name prophets there as well. So, there was maximum national, and maximum spiritual power represented at this encounter.

Moreover, these kings had the power to kill Micaiah if they didn't like what he said. And we know that King Ahab hated Micaiah, so it was a very real possibility that if Micaiah spoke a message contrary to what he wanted to hear that it could cost him his life. What would you do? What did Micaiah do?

An official of Ahab went to get Micaiah. However, this official had words of counsel for the prophet. He said, *"Behold now, the words of the prophets are uniformly favorable to the king. Please let your word be like the word of one of them, and speak favorably"* (1 Kings 22:13). Even this messenger was encouraging Micaiah to fear man instead of the Lord. How would you respond? How did Micaiah respond? He said, *"As the Lord lives, what the Lord says to me, that I shall speak"* (1 Kings 22:14). WOW!! What a response! What an example for us to follow! Micaiah chose to fear God instead of man.

This choice did cost Micaiah a high price, though. He was ridiculed, hit by one of the key prophets, and then thrown into prison and fed sparingly.

However, Micaiah prophesied that King Ahab would lose his life and the armies of Israel and Judah would be defeated. It all came to pass, and the truth of the following verse was true for Micaiah and continues to be true for us today! *"The **fear of man** brings a snare, but he who trusts in the Lord will be exalted"* (Prov. 29:25).

What was the secret to Micaiah's life? He chose to live for an audience of ONE (God), not the audience of people.

So, the question for us is this: "Will we fear man and not implement church discipline when needed, or will we fear God and do it?" If we obey, we will be exalted; if not, we'll have snares as a result. We'll have the snare of losing God's blessing in our personal lives, the snare of losing God's blessing in our churches, the

Author is OSAS
Scriptures teach not obeying leads to damnation

snare of having to give an account as leaders to God for how we "kept watch" over the flock He entrusted to us, and the snare of more sin and problems in the church.

## Fear of the Fallout

Whether we choose to implement church discipline or not, there will be fallout. There will be fallout and criticism from whatever choice we make. So, the question is: "Which kind of fallout do we want? Do we want fallout from the spiritually immature, who will likely criticize and spread rumors, or do we want fallout from God who will be displeased with us? Do we also want fallout from the spiritually mature who will see leadership tolerating sin, and possibly leave the church because they're not in agreement?

## Fear of Criticism

Those placed in church discipline most likely will cause problems and criticize leadership and the church. How do we deal with this?

I raised four boys. When they were young, they would often throw temper tantrums when they were disciplined. I chose not to give them their way no matter how angry they became.

Adults can throw temper tantrums as well. When a believer living in unrepentant sin is put in church discipline, you can count on them likely throwing a temper tantrum. Why? Because they are already filled with sin and distant from God, so we should expect a temper tantrum from them. We should also expect it from their friends and family who are spiritually immature and supporting them in their sinful lifestyle. So, the question for us is this: "Are we going to let the fear of their temper tantrum, and of those who support them, scare us away from giving them the discipline they need?"

Simply put, church discipline is discipline for adults. When we fail to discipline believers living in unrepentant sin in our church, we are allowing the fear of the fallout to govern our choice. We should never let the fear of a temper tantrum by an adult who needs church discipline scare us away from doing what we are commanded by God to do.

## It's Hard and Painful

Many individuals, churches, and church leaders choose not to deal with church discipline because it's just simply hard and painful work. It can be time-consuming, ugly, emotionally draining, and discouraging. Moreover, most people and church leaders are already too busy and don't want to take the time to deal with a negative "tar-baby."

As you well know, a tar-baby is something that is covered with tar. No matter how you try to touch it, you get dirty and messy. Sometimes this is how we feel about church discipline. It's a tar-baby. It's messy and dirty. Rather than deal with it, let's just leave it alone! However, the problem with tar-babies is that they grow. They grow in size and numbers. Remember, a little leaven affects the whole church. If we don't deal with church discipline, then we will have bigger problems to deal with later. We'll also have a "light" church that is not deep, holy, and pleasing to God. And moreover, we'll be faced with the dilemma of disobedience to God, which is an even bigger problem.

Just because something is hard and painful is no reason not to do it. Church discipline is commanded by God, and the purity of the church is one of the key responsibilities of church leaders. Leaders have no moral authority to preach about the destruction and pain sin brings if they are unwilling to implement church discipline. Moreover, they lose their right to tell others how they should obey God in the tough times if they are unwilling to obey God in their own tough time of implementing church discipline.

Johnathan Leeman says it like this:

I understand the reluctance to practice church discipline. It's a difficult matter for any number of reasons. Still, this reluctance to practice church discipline, a reluctance that many of us probably feel, may suggest that we believe ourselves to be wiser and more loving than God. God, after all, "disciplines those he loves"; and "he punishes everyone he accepts as a son" (Heb. 12:6). Do we know better than God?[20]

Additionally, Alexander Strauch provides rich insight into how difficult it is to carry out church discipline, but how it's vitally needed:

> Love is not just happy smiles or pleasant words. A critical test of genuine love is whether we are willing to confront and discipline those we care for. Nothing is more difficult than disciplining a brother or sister in Christ who is trapped in sin. It is always agonizing work—messy, complicated, often unsuccessful, emotionally exhausting, and potentially divisive. This is why most church leaders avoid discipline at all costs. But that is not love. It is lack of courage and disobedience to the Lord Jesus Christ, who Himself laid down instructions for the discipline of an unrepentant believer (Matt. 18:17–18).[21]

## It Requires Work and Clear Communication

In order to implement church discipline responsibly, it takes work and clear communication. Church leaders must be fully informed of the sin in the

---

[20] Johnathan Leeman, A Church Discipline Primer, https://www.9marks.org/article/church-discipline-primer/

[21] Alexander Strauch, Leading With Love, Lewis and Roth, 2006, p. 152, Used by Permission.

life of the sinful, unrepentant believer in their church. They must meet with affected parties and keep records of witnesses, acts, and behavior. It's no fun and requires work and time.

Leadership also should write carefully drafted statements to read before the church (and made available in written form for the church) when they arrive at steps 3 and 4 of the church discipline process: *"If he refuses to listen to them, **tell it to the church** [step 3]; and if he refuses to listen even to the church, **let him be to you as a Gentile and a tax collector** [step 4]"* (Matt. 18:17).

Carefully drafted statements provide exact clarity, a record, and are harder to be altered by gossip and misunderstanding. We'll talk more about this in chapter 16 which deals with implementing church discipline.

Because church discipline is hard work, many churches today don't do it. They just don't want the work and effort it takes. Once again, just because church discipline requires work and clear communication is no reason to disobey God and not do it.

## Church Discipline Is Viewed as Hate by Many

It's sad that the very means God has instituted for rescuing believers living in unrepentant sin from the grips of spiritual death is commonly viewed by many as hate, rather than love. What a tragedy! As a result, the "Intensive Care Unit" of most churches is out of order, and numerous believers are dying spiritual deaths because its doors are closed.

Jonathan Leeman has wise words for us to consider about love and church discipline:

> The underlying purpose in every act of discipline, of course, must be love: love for the individual, love for the church, love for the watching world, love for Christ. God, after all, "disciplines the one He loves"; and "He chastens everyone He accepts as His son" (Heb. 12:6). By abstaining from discipline, we claim that we love better than God.[22]

Most would agree that God wants us to discipline our children, so they grow up to be responsible and respectable. They understand this form of love when applied to children, yet for some reason, many Christians do just the opposite with fellow believers living in unrepentant sin. They stand by and allow them to destroy their lives, damage the testimony of the church and Christ, and do nothing. I don't believe this is true love. It might appear like love, but it allows destruction, not restoration, and how can allowing destruction be defined as love?

---

[22] Jonathan Leeman, *What are the Standards for Membership?* by Jonathan Leeman taken from Church Membership by Jonathan Leeman, copyright (2012), Crossway Books, Wheaton Illinois 60187, www.crosswaybooks.org, p. 111.

## Church Discipline Is Viewed as Judgmental

"Judge not, lest you be judged" is a misunderstood verse that seems to take precedence over any scripture that calls for discipline. Today, in our culture that has become amoral and relative, we are told we have no right to get involved in someone else's affairs, and if we do, we are crossing the line and being judgmental. According to our culture, to tell someone they are sinning is deemed as judgmental, which is a cardinal sin and unchristian. However, church discipline is a command by God that must be obeyed rather than our culture's values.

## Conclusion

There is very little church discipline today for the following reasons: (1) leadership fails to understand that the purity of the church is one of its primary roles (2) we tend to fear others rather than God (3) we fear the fallout of church discipline (4) it often brings criticism (5) it's hard and painful (6) it requires work and clear communication (7) it is generally misunderstood and viewed as hate, and (8) it is viewed as judgmental.

However, each of these difficulties is no reason to disobey God and leave sin undealt with in our churches.

# Chapter 15

## The Consequences of Not Exercising Church Discipline

Church discipline done the biblical way is the application of God's love by God's church to a believer who knows the truth but chooses to live in unrepentant sin regardless.

When a church fails to apply God's love to unrepentant believers, several consequences go into effect.

## It Reveals a Lack of Full Obedience to God by a Church and Its Leadership

2 Corinthians 2:6 says, *"Another reason I wrote you was to see if you would **stand the test and be obedient in everything**."* This verse relates to the restored believer who was put in church discipline in 1 Corinthians 5. So, it appears God also looks at church discipline as a test to see if a church and its leaders will be fully obedient to Him or not.

Implementing church discipline is probably the hardest job a church and its leadership will face. That's why it's not done much. Exercising church discipline is hard; that's why it's a test. It's a test of obedience, a test of fearing God and not man, a test of strength, and a test of will.

John MacArthur weighs in on the difficulty of carrying out church discipline and provides this wise thought:

Discipline is difficult, painful, and often heartrending. It is not that we should not love the offenders, but that we should love Christ, His church, and His Word even more. Our love to the offenders is not to be sentimental tolerance but correcting love.[23]

Administering church discipline is also a test regarding God's gift of leadership. The central core of a church's function is the teaching of God's Word to God's people. If leadership is not willing to obey God in tough matters, then they lose their right to tell the church they should as well. As a result, this core function is sacrificed, and our teaching loses its power and effectiveness.

Sadly, if members in the church see that leaders don't obey in tough matters, then they will logically conclude that they don't need to either. They will subconsciously learn that some passages should be obeyed, and some don't need to be obeyed. Consequently, they begin the path that has led many godly churches, organizations, and institutes to slowly move away from upholding God's Word to promoting messages that are contradictory to God's clear teachings.

When Scripture is compromised, and we choose what we want to obey and what we're not going to

---

[23] John MacArthur, *1 Corinthians*, Moody, 1984, p. 132.

obey, then where do we stop? We have two choices: either we fully obey Scripture regardless of the ramifications, or elevate ourselves above God, and thereby, make God subservient to us.   *idolatry*

As humans, our greatest fault since the creation until the present has been in deciding whose logic we will follow; God's or our own. God doesn't ask us to consider all the ramifications to obedience before we decide to do it. He doesn't ask us to think about the benefits or problems that might arise by using our own intelligence. Instead, He expects us to trust Him and not run all our decisions through the filter of our own human understanding: "*Trust in the Lord with all your heart and* **do not lean on your own understanding**" (Prov. 3:5).   *Amen*

*Original Sin — believe God*
*temptation to (not) believe God*

## The Church's Message Contradicts God's Message

One of the functions of church discipline is for the church to have the same message as God. If God says sin brings death, is destructive, and that He hates it, then the church should say the same. However, when a believer lives in sin and their church does nothing about it, this sends a message that sin doesn't really bring death and destruction. This is a message that contradicts what God says about sin.   *actions speak louder than words*

It's easy to preach from the pulpit about sin; it is entirely different to live it out. A church and its leadership show their commitment to God's Word by living it out, not just by talking about it. Our true test is what we do in the application, not what we say. If we fail to implement church discipline when needed, then we encourage a message that promotes hearing God's Word but not obeying it. This is a dangerous message for a congregation and its leaders to allow in their church.

## The Consequences of Sin Are Diminished

When church discipline is done properly, it warns and deters others in the church from following a sinful path. However, if those in the church see that they can live in sin, and nothing happens, then the consequences of sin are downplayed, and others are more easily led astray to engage in sin as well.

## The Purpose of Christ's Church Is Compromised

When all is said and done, Christ desires a pure bride (the church) that provides a clear message to the world of who He is, His love for all, His desire for all to know Him, and the destruction sin causes in life as a result of rejecting God and His principles for godly and healthy living. While we seek, accept, and welcome all sinning unbelievers into the church, once they are believers and represent the name of Christ, we need to hold them accountable and guard the church from impurity and sin.

If we allow believers who name the name of Christ to live in unrepentant sin, which is contrary to the message of God, and we do nothing about it, then the whole purpose of the church is compromised. We need to protect Christ's Church and call into account believers who are living in unrepentant sin. The church loses its message and purpose if it fails in this area.

John MacArthur grants a sober thought about churches that allow sin to go unchecked:

> Some churches have gotten so far away from the biblical pattern that they view church discipline as an unloving, judgmental, and divisive practice. That couldn't be further from the truth — there's nothing more loving you can do for a fellow believer in sin than to call him or her back to repentance and purity. For the sake of the individual and the rest of the church, you want to see fallen church members restored to a right relationship with Christ.[24]

### The Church Loses God's Blessing

Unfortunately, when a church fails to implement church discipline, God's heart is grieved, and He removes His full blessing upon that church. We see this

---

[24] John MacArthur, Grace to You Newsletter, April 2009, www.gty.org.

reality in the seven churches in Revelation where Jesus says He walks among them searching out their strengths and weaknesses: *"The One who holds the seven stars in His right hand, the One who walks among the seven golden lampstands"* (Rev. 2:1). The seven golden lampstands represent the seven churches (Rev. 1:20).

In the church of Ephesus, Christ threatened to remove their lampstand if they didn't obey Him and repent of their sin: *"But I have this against you, that you have left your first love. Therefore, remember from where you have fallen, and repent and do the deeds you did at first; or else I am coming to you and **will remove your lampstand out of its place** – unless you repent"* (Rev. 2:4–5). We run the risk of losing Christ's full blessing on our churches, or even losing our status as a true church altogether, when we don't obey Him in exercising church discipline. This causes me deep pause! yeah to reconsider our OSAS stance lol

The fact that Christ walked among these seven churches searching out their strengths and weaknesses should sober us up to the reality that in the same way Jesus walked among the seven churches in Revelation, He walks among our churches today analyzing our strengths and weaknesses as well. What would He say about your church? What would He say about your obedience in implementing church discipline for believers in your church living in unrepentant sin?

The accusation Christ had for the church in Ephesus was that they had left their first love. Christ affirmed how we show him our love in John 14:15: *"If you love Me, you will keep My commandments."* We leave our first love when we disobey God. Therefore, if we fail to carry out Christ's commands regarding church discipline, we fail to love God as we should. This can cause us to lose God's blessing, and possibly, our church lampstand.

J. Hampton Keathley speaks about the danger of losing God's blessing in our churches:

> Sin in the life of the church grieves the person of the Holy Spirit and quenches His power. If sin remains unchecked by the loving application of church discipline in a body of believers, the Holy Spirit must abandon such a church to its own carnal resources. The unavoidable result will be the loss of the Lord's blessing until the sin is dealt with. The defeat of Israel because of the sin of Achan in Joshua 7 illustrates the principle.[25]

Likewise, John MacArthur provides a stark warning as well:

> No church is healthy enough to resist contamination from persistent sin in its midst, any more than the healthiest and most nutritious bushel of apples can withstand contamination from even a

---

[25] J. Hampton Keathley, Church Discipline, www.bible.org, Copyright ©1996-2005

single bad one. The only solution in both cases is separation.[26]

## Spiritually Mature Believers in the Church Leave

Dealing with church discipline is not a neutral issue that has no consequences if left undone. There is going to be things that happen regardless of what we do or do not do in implementing church discipline.

If we choose to carry out church discipline, then it's likely the spiritually immature will be offended and some might leave the church.

If we choose not to carry out church discipline, then we'll likely offend the spiritually mature because they will see God's Word being disobeyed and sinful behavior being taken lightly by the church and its leadership. This, in turn, will cause some of them to leave the church.

I have seen with my own eyes the consequences of not carrying out church discipline. I saw some of the spiritually mature in a church leave because they saw serious sin in the body, but the leadership chose not to implement church discipline. *true light*

So, the question for us is this: "Who do we want to offend?" Do we want to offend the spiritually immature or the spiritually mature? Either choice we

---

[26] John MacArthur, *1 Corinthians*, Moody, 1984, p. 131.

choose has consequences. Additionally, choosing not to implement church discipline when needed also offends God.

Therefore, here's the truth and reality of the situation: if we choose to carry out church discipline, then we'll offend some of the spiritually immature in our church, and they'll leave.

However, if we choose **not** to implement church discipline, then here's the consequences: (1) we'll offend the spiritually mature and some will leave (2) we'll offend God which will cause us to lose His full blessing for our church (3) our own walk with God will be affected negatively, and (4) we'll have a weak church that has a low view of sin.

So, we need to choose which set of consequences we want and which road we want to take. I believe the only wise and obedient choice is that of obeying God and implementing church discipline when needed.

## Sin Is Viewed as Acceptable

When church discipline is passed over, then the church will have a low view of God's holiness and of the destruction and damage sin causes. If we truly believe the wages of sin is death (Rom. 3:23), then we should be concerned about holiness in our lives and churches.

Repeatedly in Scripture God warns about sin spreading among His people. He uses the term "leaven" as a symbol of this truth. As you well know, leaven is a substance used in baking which causes bread dough to rise and fluff up. All that is needed is just a tiny bit of leaven for this to happen. Therefore, God uses this example of what a little sin in the church does if we don't deal with it.

In 1 Corinthians 5:6–7, which deals with a clear example of church discipline, God uses this picture of leaven which affects the whole church: "*Your boasting is not good. Do you not know that a **little leaven leavens the whole lump of dough? Clean out the old leaven** so that you may be a new lump, just as you are in fact unleavened.*"

We see in this passage that all it takes is a little leaven (sin) in the church body that is not dealt with to spread throughout the whole church. As a result, the church will develop a spirit and mentality that sin is not really that destructive and damaging in our lives.

## Conclusion

What are the consequences of not exercising church discipline?

1. It reveals a lack of obedience to God by a church and its leaders.

2. The church's message about sin contradicts God's message about sin.

3. The consequences of sin are diminished.

4. The purpose of Christ's Church is compromised.

5. A church can lose God's blessing upon it.

6. Spiritually mature believers often leave a church when church discipline is not carried out.

7. Sin is not viewed as that destructive.

8. God is offended by our disobedience.

Martin Lloyd Jones confirms the danger of not exercising church discipline by stating:

> There is no purpose in having a basis or a confession of faith unless it is applied. So, we must assert the element of discipline as being essential to the true life of the church. And what calls itself a church which does not believe in discipline, and does not use it and apply it, is therefore not a true church.[27]

---

[27] Martin Lloyd Jones, *What is an Evangelical?* The Banner of Truth Trust, 1992, p. 83.

# Chapter 16

## How to Implement Corrective Church Discipline

## Educate Your Congregation About Church Discipline

Before church discipline is implemented, it is wise to educate the church about the role and responsibility God gives us about the process. This is a positive step and should not be viewed as negative, a bother, or unimportant.

Educating your congregation before a church discipline situation will make the implementation extremely easier. As a result, the church body will understand fully what will take place and will support leadership throughout the process. You will find that when people hear what God says about church discipline, they will get on-board quickly and stay on-board throughout the process. It will be like rolling a large ball downhill.

However, if you don't educate your church, then they won't understand what's taking place, you'll have a lot of questions and blowback, and it will be more challenging. It will be like rolling a large ball uphill.

You need to understand that a big positive of church discipline is that it wakes up the church, warns them about the dangers and destruction of sin, and purifies the church. It's all good stuff!

## Be Unified as a Leadership Team

It's vital that the leadership of the church all be unified and in agreement regarding church discipline.

It just simply won't work if they're not. This doesn't mean that one or two of the leadership team might feel more passionate and take more of a leadership role in implementing it than others, but all need to believe they are in God's will and doing what they are called to do.

Why is this important? Because when the fallout comes, and it will come, they need to be able to rest in God's will and know they are being obedient. You will need this strength in the battle. Remember, like the Prophet Micaiah; you need to live for an audience of ONE (1 Kings 22), not your emotions and what others might feel. Additionally, you'll want a unified voice to be able to answer any critics who might question your decision. If some in leadership are not on-board, then the whole matter could crumble and turn into a disaster.

*Truth trumps feelings*

## Be Organized

While it might not be fun, be sure to be organized and keep records of all the documentation about a church discipline situation. You need to responsibly answer your critics, the unrepentant sinner, the church, and others regarding this matter.

In step two of the church discipline process, Christ states the following: *"But if he does not listen to you, take one or two more with you, so that by the mouth of two or three witnesses **every fact may be confirmed**"* (Matt.

*Thank you Jesus for showing us your will now help us to carry it out faithfully*

18:16). Jesus himself tells us to establish and confirm all the facts that the witnesses tell us. So, be organized and keep track of all the facts that are confirmed.

## What Do We Do as a Small Group of Believers If Leadership Does Not Implement Church Discipline?

I believe biblically that church discipline can still be carried out in a smaller group of people (2 or 3), even if the leadership of the church chooses not to do it. This is so because as Jesus winds up His instructions on church discipline in Matthew 18, He says, *"Truly I say to you, whatever you bind on earth shall have been bound in heaven; and whatever you loose on earth shall have been loosed in heaven. Again, I say to you, that if **two of you agree** on earth about anything that they may ask, it shall be done for them by My Father who is in heaven. **For where two or three have gathered together in My name, I am there in their midst**"* (Matt. 18:18–20).

In this passage, we see that even if two or three are in agreement regarding church discipline, then Christ is in their midst responding and backing them up in this process. However, this small group should be very careful and be biblically centered. If the leadership of a church does not implement church discipline, then this small group should proceed with great caution. They should only implement church discipline if they are absolutely certain leadership is clearly being disobedient, and they have biblical support with clear facts and evidence from witnesses.

If a small group does choose to carry out church discipline after much prayer and consideration, then I believe it should be done in a private setting, just keeping everything to themselves. I don't believe it should be made public as it could undermine the authority of the church and cause bigger problems.

## Always Develop a Carefully Written Statement to Read to the Congregation

Always, always, write out a carefully drafted statement about the church discipline situation that can be read to the church by its leadership and made available for church attendees who are not present. This is extremely important to do as it ensures the church is informed in a precise, exact way. It also avoids gossip and is harder to twist or misunderstand.

At the end of the statement, it should include the signatures from the entire leadership of the church. It should not be from just the pastor or a few leaders. You need the full weight of all the leadership for maximum effect and authority.

Additionally, if any church member is asked about a church discipline situation, they can simply respond by referring to the written statement from leadership.

## When the Church Is Told About Church Discipline, Involve the Leadership

When we come to step 3 of the church discipline process and we *"Tell it to the church,"* or when we come to step 4 of the process and actually put an unrepentant believer living in sin in church discipline, it's best to have all the elders, or all the main leaders of the church, come up front and stand behind the pastor as the church is informed. This shows the church family that all of the leadership is involved and stands behind the decision. It also gives a sense of weight, authority, and professionalism to the procedure as well.

## Get Ready for Fallout

*all on the same page*
*no weakness in unity*

Fallout might come so be ready for it. Some who are put in church discipline will try to discredit the leadership of the church and the church in general. Anyone who is against them they will perceive as the enemy. This is normal and just part of the reality of the situation.

Others involved in church discipline will respond positively. Regardless of how each person put in church discipline may react, you can count on God working in the heart of the unrepentant person put in church discipline.

## Live for an Audience of One

When we looked at the story of the Prophet Micaiah (1 Kings 22), we learned that he chose to fear the Lord and not man. He stood against two kings and 400 prophets who represented the mainstream voice of their day. In other words, he stood against all the national and spiritual power of two countries (Israel and Judah, after the Kingdom of Israel was divided). He was able to do this because he chose to live for an audience of ONE (God) instead of the voices of those around him.

We will only be able to carry out church discipline, which seems to be the hardest task of a church and its leaders, if we do the same. We need to come to the place where we are biblically convinced that church discipline is the next step for a believer living in unrepentant sin, and after we are convinced we are in God's will, then we need to calmly and respectfully answer the critics who arise.

## Separate Your Feelings From God's Word

A big mistake we can make in implementing church discipline is to allow our feelings and emotions to get in the way. We can do this in two ways:

**1.** We can lean more on how we feel and say: "I feel led by the Lord to proceed with church discipline" instead of saying, "The Word of the Lord says I should move forward with church discipline." We need to move from the subjective realm in our hearts, which is based on how we feel inside, and lean more on objective facts from God's Word.

For example, if a believer living in unrepentant sin continues to choose sin, rejecting everyone who goes to them throughout the first three steps of the church discipline process, then there's no need to lean on how you feel. You lean on the clear Word of God and obey it!

**2.** We can allow personal criticisms and attacks from those in church discipline, and from others as well, affect us personally. Don't fall into this trap. It's of the Devil. Stay calm, respond to criticism biblically and respectfully, and trust in the Lord that you are simply doing what He has called you to do. Don't take anything personally!

I am reminded that those who have served God in the Bible suffered for doing so. Jeremiah is called, "The Weeping Prophet." It's believed Jeremiah also wrote the book of Lamentations, in which his weeping and laments are recorded because of the destruction of Jerusalem and the surrounding country of Israel. Like Jeremiah, it's okay to feel sorrow and grief in ministry. However, don't believe for a moment that the personal attacks directed at you, because of your obedience to God in implementing church discipline, is your fault. You are simply being a faithful servant who is carrying out your duty to God and your church. Don't let your emotions and feelings get the best of you. Stay objective; don't become subjective!

*Stay encouraged trust God in it all*

## Be Strong

Because God knew the difficulty Joshua would face in being Moses' successor and the leader of a rebellious people; He told him to be strong and courageous. We need to receive and embrace these same words that were given to Joshua when we lead in implementing church discipline:

> **Be strong and courageous**, *for you shall give this people possession of the land which I swore to their fathers to give them.* **Only be strong and very courageous**; *be careful to do according to all the law which Moses My servant commanded you; do not turn from it to the right or to the left, so that you may have success wherever you go. This book of the law shall not depart from your mouth, but you shall meditate on it day and night,* **so that you may be careful to do according to all that is written in it**; *for then you will make your way prosperous, and then you will have success. Have I not commanded you?* **Be strong and courageous**! **Do not tremble or be dismayed**, *for the Lord your God is with you wherever you go* (Josh 1:6–9).

Interestingly, God asked two things of Joshua as he began his leadership journey: (1) be strong and courageous (repeated three times), and (2) be careful to

173

obey all that is written in God's Word. This is what God asks from us today as leaders as well. Be strong and courageous and obey all my commandments. If we do this, then we will have the same promise that God gave to Joshua, "So *that you may have success wherever you go*" (Josh. 1:7). Amen

## Do We Still Implement Church Discipline if an Unrepentant Believer in Church Discipline Leaves the Church?

In most cases, the believer living in unrepentant sin will leave the church long before the final step of church discipline is implemented. This shouldn't surprise us as their heart is far from the Lord and they don't like the light of God's Word and that of His people shining into their dark heart. Does this mean we shouldn't follow through and put them in church discipline? If we shouldn't follow through because they have left the church, then little or no church discipline would ever take place.

In order to answer this question, we need to understand that there is more than one purpose for church discipline. God has given us at least seven purposes in Scripture. The restoration of a believer, as important as it is, is only one purpose of church discipline.

The other purposes like God's holiness is still important, the witness of Christ's Church to the world is still important, the purity of the church is still important, the restoration of the unrepentant believer is still important (even if they've left the church), warning other believers not to fall into similar sin is equally important, and the obedience of a church and its leaders is still important as well.

Every purpose of church discipline should be carried out even if a person leaves the church. Just because they've left doesn't change anything or any purpose. In fact, it's just one more sinful activity flowing from an unrepentant heart. *forsaking fellowship*

In each of the purposes of church discipline, we find that just because a believer living in unrepentant sin leaves the church, this changes nothing about what the purposes are for church discipline.

Therefore, yes, a resounding, yes! The process of church discipline should continue and be carried out even if an unrepentant believer leaves our church. Additionally, if we truly believe that church discipline is an act of love, then why wouldn't we continue loving and trying to win this fallen brother or sister back to the Lord even if they've left our fellowship? To do otherwise would not be genuine love!

## What About Church Hoppers in Church Discipline?

In many cases, believers who are living in unrepentant sin will leave the church when they are

confronted and go to another church. What do we do?
Here are some thoughts:

1. We should still follow through and exercise church
   discipline because there are at least seven purposes
   for it.

2. If we learn that this wayward sheep is attending
   another church, we should kindly and respectfully
   contact the pastor and let him know what has
   happened. We could also take with us the written
   statement from leadership as it will be concise, have
   the signatures of the church leaders, and provide
   authority. If the pastor listens, great! If not, then I
   would let it go. We simply can't force others to do
   what we believe is God's will.

3. At some point, we need to let believers in church
   discipline who hop from church to church go their
   way. I believe we should be careful to be
   responsible, but not police this wayward sheep. It
   will get inappropriate to follow them if they move
   from church to church. It's good to contact the first
   church they go to, but after that, I would just release
   them into the hands of God and get about the
   business of ministering in the church family we
   attend or oversee.

   In the event a person decides to attend our
   church, and we learn they are in church discipline
   from another church, then we should seek out their

former pastor and become informed. Unless the church they left is blatantly in the wrong, we should honor this church and send this sheep back home.

## What About Those Who Enable, Facilitate, or Support a Believer in Church Discipline

What do we do if believers in our church, or outside our church, enable, facilitate, or support a believer in church discipline? This is a good question and somewhat dynamic in nature. To answer this question, it will depend on several factors: (1) to what degree they are enabling, facilitating, and supporting a believer in church discipline, and (2) if they are part of, or outside of our local church fellowship.

In both cases, if any believer is facilitating or enabling another believer who is in church discipline, then this person would be described as an accomplice. This is clearly wrong and sinful. Unfortunately, in most church discipline cases, it happens.

Often, it will happen because believers don't understand how church discipline should function or they don't believe the believer who is in church discipline deserves it. Also, there are grey lines of how believers might be supporting or in contact with a believer in church discipline.

What do we do in situations like these? First, we need to separate believers who are facilitating or enabling a believer in sin who are part of our local church fellowship from believers outside our church who go to other churches.

For believers **who are part of our local church** who are enabling, facilitating, or supporting a believer in church discipline, then to be strictly biblical, we should follow the first step of Matthew 18:15, and go to them and tell them their sin. If they don't listen, then we should follow step 2 of Matthew 18:16, and take two or more (preferably from leadership because of the nature of their sin in opposing leadership). If they still don't listen, then we would follow the remaining two steps of the church discipline process with them as well.

For believers **outside** our local church who are enabling, facilitating, or supporting a believer in church discipline, then we should go to them and tell them that the person they are supporting is in church discipline and why. The statement from leadership that was read to the church could be used at this time to bring clarity and authority. If they refuse to listen and choose to continue supporting this person in church discipline after we utilized steps 1 and 2 of Matthew 18:15–16, then I believe we just need to stop at this point because we can't carry out steps 3 and 4 of Matthew 18:17, because they are not part of our local church.

## Be Careful About Policing

I would try to avoid policing how everyone should treat another believer in church discipline. This can get tricky and awkward. If there are believers who are clearly enabling, facilitating, or supporting a believer in church discipline, then I think biblically speaking we should at least go to them, but in cases that are smaller and not so clearly defined, I would suggest we just leave them alone, pray, and let God work things out.

It should be made clear from the leadership of the church how others should treat a person in church discipline, but once again, if everyone doesn't do it exactly as they should in the small details, I wouldn't worry about it too much. I would only focus on the big cases.

## How Do Family Members Living With a Believer in Church Discipline Relate to Him or Her?

For family members who are living in the same home with a believer in church discipline, things will be different with them than with believers outside the home. This is so because they will still have to have contact and interact with their family member in church discipline because they live together.

However, I believe family members living in the same home with a believer in church discipline should clearly express that they support the church discipline and are not going to enable, facilitate, or support them in any way.

## Legal Concerns

We live in a sue-happy day, and it's possible some put in church discipline might retaliate. In order to prevent this, many churches are asking their members to sign a membership agreement wherein they agree to be put in church discipline if they decide to live in unrepentant sin. However, even if we don't have an agreement in writing, or don't have church membership, I would still obey God and do what Scripture teaches. At some point, we just need to trust God and be willing to suffer the consequences for obedience to Him.

## What About Churches That Don't Have Membership?

A growing amount of churches today don't have membership. How do we carry out church discipline in these kinds of churches?

Even if we don't have membership, there will generally always be four kinds of people in our church: (1) the strong, faithful sheep attendees (2) regular sheep attendees (3) visitors who are saved, and (4) visitors who are not saved.

I believe we have the responsibility to fulfill the church discipline process for all who are the strong faithful or regular attendees, and we don't need a formal document to do this.

For the visitors who are believers, we would proceed with caution discerning how we should deal with them if they are living in unrepentant sin. And for the unsaved visitors, we would just love and accept them as Christ did on earth, ministering the Word to them in hopes they will repent and receive Christ as their Lord and Savior.

Formal documents of membership will give us more legal protection if church discipline must be carried out, but just because we might not have membership, or a legally signed document, does not mean we're relieved of the command Christ gives us to carry out church discipline. God's Word will always supersede any human document, or the lack thereof.

## Don't Move Too Fast or Too Slow

It's important to give an unrepentant believer time to repent, but in all reality, it doesn't take that much time to do so.

When John the Baptist and Jesus preached about repentance, they didn't suggest that a person wait a long time in order to make a decision. I believe it's the same with believers living in unrepentant sin. The simple question before them is: "Are you going to repent and obey God, yes or no?"

Many times in Scripture we hear these words, *"Today if you hear His voice, do not harden your hearts"* (Heb. 3:15). These are the same words an unrepentant believer needs to heed. Today, today is the time to repent. Not in a week, a month, or six months if you feel like it. *you probgrened The Sprint by Then*

Now I am not promoting rushing through the church discipline process, but I think Scripture supports a movement that is much faster than what most believe and exercise. Why? Because as mentioned, repentance shouldn't take a long time according to Scripture.

When Christ outlined the process of church discipline, He did not give a timetable. He just outlined the steps. The process of church discipline, according to Jesus, could be implemented easily in a few weeks or so.

In 1 Corinthians 5, where we have the clearest example of church discipline, Paul severely rebuked the Corinthian church for the lack of church discipline and said:

> *For I, on my part, though absent in body but present in spirit, have already judged him who has so committed this, as though I were present. In the name of our Lord Jesus, when you are assembled, and I with you in spirit, with the power of our Lord Jesus, I have decided to deliver such a one to Satan for the destruction of his*

*flesh, so that his spirit may be saved in the day of the Lord Jesus* (1 Cor. 5:3–5).

In this case, church discipline was not a long process but happened right away. *also with paul not even being there*

My experience as a pastor and missionary has shown me that most church discipline is carried out too slow and too late. This might be the case because in much of my research in writing this book, a slow process for implementing church discipline was promoted. However, I simply don't see this in Scripture.

We must understand that there is a hardening of a believer's heart the longer they live in sin. Therefore, the longer the process of church discipline takes, the greater the chance this person will never repent because their heart grows callous. *"For the heart of this people **has become dull**, with **their ears they scarcely hear**, and **they have closed their eyes**, otherwise they would see with their eyes, hear with their ears, and understand with their heart and return, and I would heal them"* (Matt. 13:15). Also, the longer an unrepentant believer living in sin continues in their sin, the greater the destruction they cause themselves and those around them.

When we move too slow in church discipline, we also give room for gossip. Why is this so? Because information moves on a sublevel among the church and outsiders rather than coming in a concise form from church leadership, which in turn, can warn the church not to gossip about the matter. In fact, gossip is no longer a temptation for most as they now know the facts.

I also believe one of the reasons we might move so slow in church discipline is because it's hard and painful, and therefore, we just frankly don't want to deal with the problem. It's really a form of procrastination and irresponsibility, not a desire to rightly interpret God's Word and obey Him.

## Conclusion

In order to implement church discipline wisely and biblically, we should do the following: (1) educate our people (2) be unified as leadership (3) be organized and confirm the facts (4) develop a carefully written statement (5) manage the fallout wisely (6) live for an audience of One (7) separate our feelings from objective truth (8) be strong, and (9) not drag out the church discipline process too long.

# Chapter 17

## Church Discipline Should Not Be Abusive

## Church Discipline Must Be Done Right

Church discipline, or also known as corrective discipline, should never be carried out in an abusive way. It's vital we understand this danger because, unfortunately, this is how it's been carried out in some situations.

Because of abusive cases of church discipline, when many Christians, and even non-Christians think about this issue, it can conjure up a sense of horror. Fred Greco states it well:

Church Discipline — the very phrase seems to bring to the minds of most Christians a parade of horrors. It seems like our current image of church discipline is that of repressive, out-of-touch tyrants telling us everything that we may and may not do. This is not surprising when we consider the public incidents of abuse of authority both inside and outside the church. There is also the idea that church discipline appears out of touch with our modern understanding of Christian liberty, an understanding in which the individual Christian is his own judge in all matters regarding the Christian faith and the Christian life.[28]

In some cases of church discipline, there have been abuses and wrong motives which have led to a

---

[28] Fred Greco, Church Discipline,
https://www.ligonier.org/learn/articles/church-discipline/, accessed 02/18/2019.

misunderstanding of how God intended for church discipline to be carried out. Church discipline carried out in a biblical way is a pathway of blessing, restoration, healing, and deepening. It should not be viewed as negative, but as God meant it to be, something positive.

## Church Discipline Should Be Done in Love

The goal of church discipline is to rescue and restore an unrepentant believer living in sin. It is not to publicly humiliate them, retaliate against them, control them with impure motives, or win a personal battle or fight with them. *yes*

If church discipline is not carried out with a reverent, respectful, and loving spirit, then God will not honor it, and the church will not follow in the process of implementing it.

Galatians 6:1, provides the right attitude we should have in the church discipline process: *"Brethren, even if anyone is caught in any trespass, you who are spiritual, restore such a one in a spirit of gentleness; each one looking to yourself, so that you too will not be tempted."*

## Church Discipline Should Not Be Done Out of Bitterness

It is very likely that the unrepentant believer living in sin has caused pain, suffering, damage, and hardship to individuals, the church, and its leadership.

This, in turn, can cause church discipline to be done in a bitter and abusive manner. This is not the biblical approach and should be rejected. Each person involved in rescuing and restoring a believer in the church discipline process should guard their hearts, and not allow a root of bitterness to spring up within them and become defiled. *"See to it that no one comes short of the grace of God; that **no root of bitterness springing up causes trouble, and by it many be defiled"** (Heb. 12:15).*

## Church Discipline Should Be Bathed in Prayer

Church leadership, and all involved in rescuing a fallen believer should humbly be seeking God and praying throughout the entire church discipline process. From the moment it comes to their attention, seeking God's will and guidance through prayer and His Word should be a priority.

Our prayers should include praying for the unrepentant believer we're seeking to rescue and restore, praying for the church, praying for ourselves, praying that only God's perfect will would be done, and that Satan and our fleshly desires would have no part in the process. Our prayers can follow the guidelines found in the following verses:

*This is the confidence which we have before Him, that, if we ask anything according to His will, He hears us. And if we know that He hears us in whatever we ask, we know that we have the requests which we have asked from Him* (1 John 5:14–15).

*With all prayer and petition pray at all times in the Spirit, and with this in view, be on the alert with all perseverance and petition for all the saints* (Eph. 6:18).

## We Should Be Humble

Rescuing and restoring a fallen brother or sister should be approached with humility and respect. There is no place for pride, self-righteousness, harshness, or condescendence.

Pride can ruin and contaminate the whole process of restoration: *"When pride comes, then comes dishonor, but with the humble is wisdom"* (Prov. 11:2). Therefore, we should prayerfully guard against pride at all cost.

We should also show the same attitude of humility that we would desire if we were in need of being rescued and restored. *"Therefore I, the prisoner of the Lord, implore you to walk in a manner worthy of the calling with which you have been called, **with all humility and gentleness, with patience, showing tolerance for one another in love"** (Eph. 4:1–2).

## We Must Be Transparent and Right With God

We cannot fulfill God's will in rescuing and restoring a believer living in sin if we aren't right with God and in fellowship with Him. We must realize that in some regards we are entering enemy territory. A fallen believer living in sin has allowed their fleshly desires and the Devil to deceive and hold them captive in their sin. To be effective for God, we must be right with Him and filled with His Spirit. Therefore, understanding God's will in how to best minister to a fallen believer is paramount. 2 Timothy 2:24–26, provides God's wisdom for how we can do this effectively:

> *The Lord's bond-servant must* **not be quarrelsome,** *but be* **kind to all, able to teach, patient when wronged, with gentleness correcting those who are in opposition,** *if perhaps God may grant them repentance leading to the knowledge of the truth, and they may come to their senses and* **escape from the snare of the devil,** *having been held captive by him to do his will.*

## Conclusion

Unfortunately, there have been cases of abuse in attempting to rescue and restore a believer living in sin. However, just because some have done it wrong does not mean we should not do it. For example, just because some people use the Internet for sinful purposes does not mean others cannot use it for good. Rescuing a fallen believer is the same.

In order to rescue and restore a fallen believer, we should do it in love, without bitterness, with much prayer and supplication, in humility, and by being right with God and in fellowship with Him.

# Chapter 18

## How to Handle Gossip in Church Discipline

Gossip can be an issue if church discipline is not handled and implemented correctly. Many people think that if church discipline is carried out that the church will run the risk of having gossip as a part of the process.

The truth is that gossip already exists in most situations anyway. In fact, there is generally more gossip when church discipline is not carried out because the sinful activities of those sinning become known to most people in the church by being spread at a sub-level, instead of coming directly and clearly from leadership via a written statement.

It's also helpful and important for leadership to warn the church about the dangers of gossip and not to engage in it as they move through the church discipline process.

## What Is Gossip?

Gossip is engaging in conversation about a certain issue in which I am not a part of the biblical solution. It is a negative spirit that is intent on hurting someone instead of prayerfully helping them. It is a person who has information about someone, or a situation, and shares it with others who have no business in the matter. It is delighting in sharing information with the intent of slandering and dishonoring another person.

## What Is Not Gossip?

It needs to be made very clear that any information shared with the leadership of the local church should not be considered gossip. The leadership has the responsibility to carry out church discipline, and they can't do it without being adequately informed.

Therefore, what is shared with the leadership is not gossip because God gives the duty to leadership to carry out church discipline. And as mentioned, leadership must have truthful and accurate information to do this. If information is withheld from them because some might think it's gossip, then the leadership will not be able to responsibly carry out church discipline as they are commanded to do.

## How to Prevent Gossip

Always, always, write out a carefully drafted statement about the church discipline situation that can be read to the church by church leadership, and copies of this statement made available to the church, and those who are not present. This ensures that you inform the church in a precise, exact way. At the end of the statement, it should include the signatures from the entire leadership of the church. It should not be from just the pastor or a few leaders.

Carefully drafted statements provide exact clarity, a record, and are harder to be altered by gossip and misunderstanding. This is extremely important to do.

Moreover, if any church attendee is asked by someone about a church discipline situation, they can simply refer to the written statement from leadership. This will greatly remove the tendency for people to gossip.

When we move too slow in church discipline, we also give room for gossip. Why is this so? Because information moves on a sub-level among the church and outsiders rather than coming in a concise form from church leadership, which in turn, can warn the church not to gossip about the matter. Actually, gossip is no longer a temptation for most after they are presented with the facts.

## Conclusion

Gossip is engaging in conversation about a certain issue in which I am not a part of the biblical solution. It is a negative spirit that is intent on hurting someone instead of prayerfully helping them.

It should be made clear that any information shared with the leadership of the local church should not be considered gossip as the leadership has the responsibility to carry out church discipline, and they can't do it without being adequately informed.

Gossip can be prevented by informing the church in a concise written statement read by leadership and by warning them not to engage in any form of it.

# Chapter 19

## The Results of Corrective Church Discipline

## God Works in a Unique Way

God has designed the process of church discipline to result in an unrepentant believer living in sin to return to the Lord. To you and me, this may seem like a harsh way to accomplish this purpose. However, because fellowship is such a deep need for believers, and because God has made us social creatures, in His wisdom He uses the body of Christ to play a key role in working with Himself in carrying out church discipline.

God also works in a unique way in the life of a believer in church discipline, often sending them troubles, dryness of soul, physical issues, and so forth. These troubles will be clearly seen as from the Lord if the church cooperates with God by placing an unrepentant believer in church discipline. However, if the church does not participate with God by obeying Him in this area, then God's work will be diminished and not as clearly seen. God can still work, but His work is not as visible to the sinful believer and the rest of the church.

*[handwritten margin note: His God sends Plagues / his people will turn to Him]*

*[handwritten note: Don't Stand in His way ! / be a vessel of honor not dishonor]*

## Church Discipline Works

Some would argue that church discipline is not needed or doesn't work in bringing an unrepentant believer back into the fold, but the Bible clearly tells us it does! Notice Paul's words to the church in Corinth after they obeyed his instructions to exercise church discipline on a man who was living in unrepentant sin in 1 Corinthians 5, and as a result, he repented and was restored.

*"The punishment inflicted on him by the majority is sufficient for him. Now instead, you ought to forgive and comfort him, so that he will not be overwhelmed by excessive sorrow. I urge you, therefore, to reaffirm your love for him"* (2 Cor. 2:6–7).

What a wonderful example God has given us for how church discipline should work! The Corinthian believers obeyed God and their spiritual leaders by putting this immoral man in church discipline and expelling him from the church. God used their obedience, combined with His work in this man's heart, to bring him to repentance and restoration. Paul then instructed them on how to receive him back. They were to forgive him, comfort him, and reaffirm their love for him. This same procedure should guide the church today in dealing with Christians caught in sin.

We cannot say we love a fallen believer living in sin if we choose not to implement church discipline. In essence, when we don't exercise church discipline, we are saying by our actions that we do not love a sinning believer and don't really care about him or her.

Unfortunately, rather than attempt to rescue brothers and sisters in the grips of sin, most evangelical churches just let them go their own way in hopes they might find their way back to God and His fold. However, few ever do, and in the meantime, their sinful choices leave a wake of destruction in their own lives, and in the lives of those around them.

## Church Discipline Saves From a Multitude of Sins

James 5:19–20, sums up the purpose of church discipline perfectly: *"My brethren, if any among you strays from the truth and one turns him back, let him know that he who turns a sinner from the error of his way **will save his soul from death and will cover a multitude of sins**."* When we exercise church discipline in the life of a believer living in unrepentant sin, we save their souls from death. We also save them, and those around them, from a multitude of sins.

Rescuing a wayward believer is the same principle found in the parable of the lost sheep: *"What man among you, if he has a hundred sheep and **has lost one of them**, does not leave the ninety-nine in the open pasture and go after the one which is lost **until he finds it? When he has found it, he lays it on his shoulders, rejoicing"*** (Luke 15:4–5).

Christ certainly didn't leave lost sheep to fend for themselves, hopefully to stumble back to the Shepherd and His fold. Instead, He sought the lost sheep, and that's exactly what we should do with the lost sheep who are living in unrepentant sin in our midst. We should seek them out, trying with all our heart to rescue them, and if needed, using God's loving plan of church discipline.

## A Healthy and Pure Church

On certain occasions in Scripture, God sets precedents to communicate a clear and vital message He wants us to understand. In order to communicate the dangers of sin and disobedience in the community of the young Jewish nation as they were embarking on the conquest of the Promised Land, He used the sin of Achan as a stark precedent and example in Joshua 7:1:

> But the sons of Israel acted unfaithfully in regard to the things under the ban, for Achan, the son of Carmi, the son of Zabdi, the son of Zerah, from the tribe of Judah, took some of the things under the ban, **therefore the anger of the Lord burned against the sons of Israel**.

Achan took possessions from the conquest of Jericho that God had forbidden. As a result, the Israelites were defeated in battle against the much smaller town of Ai, which caused the nation to lose innocent lives. As a result, God commanded that Achan, along with his whole family, were to be killed. God did this to send a powerful message to the Israelites that He would not allow sin to go unchecked among them. They were a community and the sin of one person affected everyone in the community.

God, once again, set a sobering precedent in the early church as well when He took the lives of Ananias and Sapphira for lying to the Holy Spirit regarding the sale of their property, and how much of it they donated to the church. We find this tragic account in Acts 5:

> *Why is it that you have conceived this deed in your heart? You have not lied to men but to God. And as he heard these words, Ananias fell down and breathed his last;* **and great fear came over all who heard of it.** *The young men got up and covered him up, and after carrying him out, they buried him* (Acts 5:4–6).

Later, Sapphira, the wife of Ananias, died as well for lying and saying the same thing as her husband.

God used this precedent to send a powerful message to the Early Church that He would not allow sin in their midst. His church was to be holy so that it could send a clear message to the world about who God is and the abundant life He offers through the gospel. This abundant life cannot include sin as the wages of sin is death and destruction.

In part, as a result of God's judgment in taking the lives of Ananias and his wife, fear fell upon everyone, and the church began to explode with growth: "*And all the more believers in the Lord,* **multitudes of men and women, were constantly added to their number**" (Acts 5:14).

## A Strong Church for Fulfilling the Great Commission

When believers live like the unsaved, they lose their power and message in sharing the gospel. The unsaved see no difference in how they live and the saved live. However, when believers live serious, devoted lives to Christ, then the world takes notice. *w/o holiness none shall see God*

One of the most used weapons by Satan and the world is the hypocrisy of believers. We claim to be Christians but allow sin to go unchecked. This diminishes the power of the gospel. Therefore, when a church allows believers to live in unrepentant sin and does nothing, it gives the enemy solid ground to attack and destroy Christ's message of salvation. However, when the church carries out church discipline, it removes the accusations Satan and the world can rightfully use against it.

Mark Dever speaks about how church discipline actually helps in evangelism and the fulfillment of the Great Commission:

> Church discipline is a powerful tool in evangelism. People notice when our lives are different, especially when there's a whole community of people whose lives are different—not people whose lives are perfect, but whose lives are marked by genuinely trying to love God and love one another. When churches are seen as conforming to the world, it makes our evangelistic task all the more

*Hypocrisy slanders the name of God to the Gentiles Rom. 2*

difficult. As Nigel Lee of English InterVarsity once said, we become so like the unbelievers they have no questions they want to ask us. May we so live that people are made constructively curious.[29]

## Conclusion

Church discipline works! We see a clear example of this in 1 Corinthians 5, and 2 Corinthians 2.

We also see that God uses strong precedents on occasion throughout Scripture to teach vital and necessary lessons to His people. He did this in the Old Testament in the book of Joshua, and He did it in the New Testament in the book of Acts. In both cases, God was providing a powerful warning regarding the role of sin in His people. Sin causes death, so He did all He could to set strong precedents against it.

It is one thing to sin and repent; this is the normal process of growth in Christ for all believers. However, it is entirely different to choose to live in sin and refuse to repent. For believers in this state, God commands us to implement church discipline in their lives with the hope of rescuing and restoring them.

When we have healthy and pure churches, our ability to evangelize and fulfill the Great Commission greatly increases.

---

[29] Mark Dever, *Nine Marks of a Healthy Church*, Crossway, 2000, p. 176.

# Chapter 20

# When and How Does Church Discipline End?

When and how does church discipline end? Church discipline ends the moment a believer who is in church discipline repents with true biblical sorrow for their sin. In some cases, this repentance might include making amends and restitution.

In cases where a believer in church discipline does not repent, then there is no time limit for ending church discipline, and it should stay in place until the person either repents of their sin or dies. *"I have decided to deliver such a one to Satan for the **destruction of his flesh**, so that his spirit may be saved in the day of the Lord Jesus"* (1 Cor. 5:5).

## It's Been a Heart Problem

It's helpful to understand that the central problem in the life of a believer living in unrepentant sin has been a heart problem. At the core of their being, they have chosen to reject God's will for them and follow their own fleshly desires and will. Their problem has dealt with who has been on the throne and lord of their lives; God, or themselves. Christ said that no one could serve two masters. We always face a choice in our lives of who we're going to serve, our own fleshly desires, or the desires of Christ.

A believer who has been living in unrepentant sin has come to the place of allowing their heart to become hard, calloused, dull of hearing, and seared. deluded

Unless the heart of a believer who has been living in unrepentant sin is changed, then their problems will not be fixed, and true change will not occur. They need the power and grace of God in their lives, and this power and grace come only through humility and repentance. There's no power in people's great advice, wisdom, and suggestions, as important as they may be. Advice and wisdom only help if there is a true change of heart and the unrepentant believer is willing to humble themselves before the Lord in order to receive His grace and power for true and lasting change in their lives. There is simply no hope without submitting to God and His will for them.

## What Does Genuine, Biblical Repentance Look Like?

Because a believer who has been living in sin was placed in church discipline, this reveals the state of their heart. They chose not to repent and obey God on their own but had to be forced to do this. Therefore, there will always be a need to discern the sincerity of this person's repentance. Once again, it's vital that we understand this fact and prayerfully discern the sincerity of repentance in the life of a believer who has been living in sin for some time.

Because genuine repentance is so crucial, let's look at God's Word and allow Him to tell us what it looks like.

sackcloth +ashes
a 180° turn in life
action, change   205
greif over their wickedness

## 1. Biblical Repentance Acknowledges and Confesses Sin

Psalm 32:4–5: *"For day and night Your hand was heavy upon me; my vitality was drained away as with the fever heat of summer. **I acknowledged my sin to You, and my iniquity I did not hide**; I said, '**I will confess my transgressions to the Lord**'; and You forgave the guilt of my sin."*

Those demonstrating biblical repentance will acknowledge and confess their sins to the Lord. If this is not done seriously and completely, then genuine repentance likely has not occurred.

## 2. Biblical Repentance Is Sorrowful and Obedient

2 Corinthians 7:8–11: *For though **I caused you sorrow** by my letter, I do not regret it; though I did regret it — for I see that that letter caused you **sorrow**, though only for a while I now rejoice, not that you were made **sorrowful**, but that you were made **sorrowful to the point of repentance**; for you were made **sorrowful according to the will of God**, so that you might not suffer loss in anything through us. **For the sorrow that is according to the will of God produces a repentance without regret**, leading to salvation, but the sorrow of the world produces death. For behold what earnestness this very thing, this **godly sorrow**, has produced in you: what **vindication** of yourselves, what **indignation**, what **fear**, what **longing**, what **zeal**, what **avenging of wrong**!"*

We see that biblical, godly sorrow will have vindication (being cleared of wrong), indignation (repudiation of sin), fear (fear of the Lord and what He thinks), longing (desiring that which is good), zeal (passion to serve and obey God), and avenging of wrong (restitution and restoration of wrongs committed). Biblical repentance is sorrow bathed in action and change, not just feeling bad.

## 3. Biblical Repentance Is Humble, Submissive, and Mournful

James 4:6–10: *"Therefore, it says, 'God is opposed to the proud, but gives grace to the humble.' Submit therefore to God. Resist the devil and he will flee from you. Draw near to God and He will draw near to you. Cleanse your hands, you sinners; and purify your hearts, you double-minded. Be miserable and mourn and weep; let your laughter be turned into mourning and your joy to gloom. Humble yourselves in the presence of the Lord, and He will exalt you."*

Biblical repentance includes humility, submission to God, drawing near to God, cleansing, forsaking sin, purity of heart, mourning and sorrow, and weeping and gloom over sins committed. Repentance that does not genuinely include these attitudes is questionable.

when I was restored I could barely speak. I was overwhelmed for weeks because I knew I deserved hell + God is so merciful

207

## 4. Biblical Repentance Bears Fruit and Works

James 2:14–18, 26: *"What use is it, my brethren, if someone says he has faith,* **but he has no works?** *Can that faith save him? If a brother or sister is without clothing and in need of daily food, and one of you says to them, 'Go in peace, be warmed and be filled,' and yet you do not give them what is necessary for their body, what use is that?* **Even so, faith, if it has no works, is dead, being by itself.** *But someone may well say, 'You have faith, and I have works; show me your faith without the works, and* **I will show you my faith by my works.'** **For just as the body without the spirit is dead, so also faith without works is dead.**"

Biblical repentance should bear fruit and works, or it's likely not genuine.

## Unique Situations Regarding When Church Discipline Ends

Some situations are different than others regarding when and how you end church discipline. For example, when a person is separated or involved in divorcing their spouse for unbiblical reasons, they should be put in church discipline. However, when their divorce is over, and they have remarried, then you still strive to see a repentant heart, but you cannot demand that they divorce their new spouse and remarry their old one. That would not be biblical. This truth is found in the following passage:

*"When a man takes a wife and marries her, and it happens that she finds no favor in his eyes because he has found some indecency in her, and he writes her a certificate of divorce and puts it in her hand and sends her out from his house, and she leaves his house and goes and becomes another man's wife, and if the latter husband turns against her and writes her a certificate of divorce and puts it in her hand and sends her out of his house, or if the latter husband dies who took her to be his wife,* **then her former husband who sent her away is not allowed to take her again to be his wife,** *since she has been defiled; for that is an abomination before the Lord, and you shall not bring sin on the land which the Lord your God gives you as an inheritance"* (Deut. 24:1–4).

So, in a situation like this, it would be unbiblical to demand that a spouse divorce their new spouse to take back their old one. However, if they do not repent of their former sin, then we would leave them in church discipline. If they do repent of their past sin, then we have no other alternative but to move on, take the person where they're at, and work to restore their life. But we should always remember that church discipline consistently ends with repentance.

## Conclusion

Because a believer who has been living in sin was placed in church discipline, this reveals the state of their heart. They chose not to repent and obey God on their own but had to be forced to do this. Therefore, there will always be a need to discern the sincerity of this person's repentance.

Unless the heart of a believer who has been living in unrepentant sin is changed, then their problems will not be fixed, and true change will not occur. They need the power and grace of God in their lives. This power and grace will be made abundant to them when genuine and sincere repentance takes place.

Biblical repentance should include humility, submission to God, drawing near to God, cleansing, forsaking sin, purity of heart, mourning and sorrow, and weeping and gloom over sins committed. Biblical repentance also should bear fruit and works, or it's not genuine. Repentance that does not genuinely include these attitudes is questionable.

Church discipline ends the moment sincere repentance occurs in the life of a believer in church discipline. When this happens, believers and the church should rush in to restore them, welcome them back, and shower them with relational love and fellowship.

The attitude of believers and the church during this time of exercising church discipline is like that of the father of the prodigal son. We pray for them, we wait for them, and we look for them. The moment they return, then we welcome them back, kill the fatted calf, and rejoice that a brother lost has returned.

# Chapter 21

## Restoring and Rebuilding
## Fallen Believers

## Mentoring

In order for there to be ongoing growth and change in the life of a believer who has been living in unrepentant sin, mentoring will play a vital role. This believer has come out of a period of hardness and disobedience to the Lord, and they will need help rebuilding their spiritual discipline and devotion.

During this time, they will need to learn to put-off old habits and ways of thinking, and put-on new habits and ways of thinking. It's a rebuilding time in their life.

## What Is Mentoring?   *disapuship*

Biblical mentoring is an informal relationship wherein a more spiritually mature person teaches and models godly, life-skills to others who are generally less spiritually mature. It can be formal, informal, take place in a group setting, take place in an individual setting, can be regular, or somewhat sporadic.

Examples of mentoring include small group Bible studies, Sunday School classes, youth group, one on one discipleship studies, accountability partners, counseling sessions, and so forth.

The most effective mentoring takes place in a one on one setting, or in a small group where specific truths and life-skills are intentionally passed on.

## Mentoring Provides an Example

Christ was a rabbi who modeled what He taught to His disciples. This was done as they spent time together, took trips together, lived together for periods of time, and served together. After learning from Christ, His disciples would then practice what they learned.

We see mentoring as a central focus for teaching and training in other examples from Scripture as well: Moses mentored Joshua, Naomi mentored Ruth, Elijah mentored Elisha, and Paul mentored Timothy. After Paul had mentored Timothy, he encouraged Timothy to mentor others: *"You then, my child, be strengthened by the grace that is in Christ Jesus, and what you have heard from me in the presence of many witnesses entrust to faithful men who will be able to teach others also"* (2 Tim. 2:1).

## Accountability

A restored believer coming out of church discipline will also need accountability. This can come from a number of people such as their mentor, pastor, friend, church leader, and so forth.

In an article by Gordon Tredgold, Founder and CEO of Leadership Principles, he says the following about the value and purpose of accountability:

You can't just tell people they're accountable, and then leave them to it. Yes, it may work for some, but not for all. You need to set up review sessions; you have to check in and see how people are doing. This serves three purposes: (1) It lets them know that they will be held accountable for the activities. (2) It gives you an opportunity to provide support in case things start to go awry. (3) It offers you the opportunity to offer praise and encouragement to move people further if things are going well. Accountability is something that has to be worked at. There has to be a clear and consistent strategy on how it's going to be implemented and validated.[30]

## Discipleship

A restored believer coming out of church discipline will also need intensive discipleship. There should be put in place some kind of plan for this that will last for some time. Now while discipleship is an ongoing process in all our lives that should never end, I'm referring to a specialized kind of discipleship that addresses the specific needs of a restored believer coming out of church discipline.

This can be carried out by a mentor, pastor, friend, church leader, etc.

---

[30] Gordon Tredgold, *7 Truths About Accountability That You Need To Know*, https://www.inc.com, https://www.inc.com/gordon-tredgold/7-truths-about-accountability-that-you-need-to-kno.html, Accessed 12/15/2-18.

Dallas Willard, in his book, *The Great Omission,* makes an incredible observation regarding the importance of discipleship when stating that the word "disciple" occurs 269 times in the New Testament, but "Christian" is only found three times.[31] Willard defines discipleship as the foundational aspect of what it means to be saved and be a true follower of Christ.

Anthony Robinson, in his article "Follow Me," picks up on Willard's statement and believes that because the word "disciple" occurs 269 times in the New Testament, it defines the mark of a genuine believer.[32] Robinson also contends that the church today is focusing primarily on conversion and neglecting the way of life here and now, which is discipleship.[33]

## What Is Discipleship?

Discipleship is the process of becoming like Christ in our nature, character, values, purposes, thoughts, knowledge, attitudes, and will. In other words, it's the process of becoming spiritually mature. It lasts a lifetime and isn't relegated to a temporary study or

---

[31] Dallas Willard, *The Great Omission* (HarperCollins, Kindle Edition, 2009-10-13), p. 3.

[32] Anthony B. Robinson, *The Renewed Focus on Discipleship: 'Follow Me'* (Christian Century, 124 no 18 S 4 2007, pp. 23-25. Publication Type: Article. ATLA Religion Database with ATLASerials. Hunter Resource Library), p. 23, Accessed 12/10/2014.

[33] Ibid., p. 23.

dedicated class taken for a time and ended. Bill Hull claims, "It's not a program or an event; it's a way of life. Discipleship is not for beginners alone; it's for all believers for every day of their lives."[34]

## Discipleship Is the Only Way to Reach Spiritual Maturity

Discipleship is the vehicle God uses to make us spiritually mature. There is no other way! It's the pathway we must follow to be transformed into the image of Christ and reach spiritual maturity. Through discipleship, God grants us life, love, joy, peace, healthy minds, healthy relationships, healthy families, and healthy churches. It's our life's calling and the highest purpose to which we can give ourselves.

Howard Hendricks went so far as to claim, "When a person makes a profession of faith and ... is never taken through a formal discipleship process, then there's little hope of seeing genuine spiritual transformation."[35]

To the degree we are committed to discipleship will be the degree to which we attain spiritual maturity. To the degree we neglect our commitment to discipleship

---

[34] Bill Hull, *The Complete Book of Discipleship: On Being and Making Followers of Christ* (The Navigators Reference Library 1, 2014, NavPress, Kindle Edition), Kindle Locations 436-437.

[35] C. S. Lewis Institute, *Sparking a Discipleship Movement in America and Beyond,* cslewisinstitute.org, http://www.cslewisinstitute.org/webfm_send/210, Accessed 08/19/2015.

will be the degree to which we suffer destruction, devastation, and eternal loss.

## The Role of Discipleship in the Ministry of Christ

I've had the splendid privilege of standing on the mountain where it's believed Christ gave the Great Commission. It's called Mt. Arbel and has a spectacular view of the Sea of Galilee. It's estimated that Jesus spent 70% of His ministry time around the Sea of Galilee, so Mt. Arbel would have been the perfect backdrop for Christ to have spoken some of His last and most important words to His disciples: "*Go therefore and* **make disciples** *of all nations, baptizing them in the name of the Father and of the Son and of the Holy Spirit, teaching them to observe all that I have commanded you. And behold, I am with you always, to the end of the age*" (Matt. 28:19–20).

A large part of Christ's earthly ministry entailed making disciples. During this time, He invested heavily into 12 men. Then, upon leaving, He commanded these men to go into all the world and make disciples.

The Great Commission Mandate given by Christ contains the summation of His purpose for the original disciples and all believers for all time. It would make sense then that the essential components of the discipleship-making process should be fully understood and obeyed. Unfortunately, there appears to be an immense lack of understanding in this vital area, and the gap between the command and implementation is alarmingly wide.

## The Role of Discipleship in the Ministry of the Apostles

In addition to Christ's Great Commission Mandate to make disciples, the Apostle Paul sums up his, and the other Apostles' life work with the following statement: *"Him we proclaim, warning everyone and teaching everyone with all wisdom that we may **present everyone mature in Christ**. For this I toil, struggling with all his energy that he powerfully works within me"* (Col. 1:28–29). This verse highlights the central purpose and work of the Apostles, which was to present every person spiritually mature in Christ.

Because presenting every person mature in Christ would logically incorporate discipleship, and because the Apostles took Christ's command seriously to make disciples, it's safe to say that the summation of the Apostles' work was discipleship as well.

Therefore, in the Great Commission, we see the summation of Christ's work and purpose, and in Colossians 1:28–29, we see the summation of the Apostles' work and purpose, each focusing on discipleship as its central theme. For this reason, the role of discipleship is paramount in the life of every believer and church if we're going to be serious about becoming spiritually mature.

For the believer who has been in church discipline, they will need more help than most in reaching spiritual maturity. Intensive, specialized discipleship is the answer for them.

## Fellowship

A restored believer coming out of church discipline must also recommit themselves to church attendance and fellowship with other believers. They need the encouragement of others, the ministry of the Word of God in their life, accountability, and counsel. Just like every other believer, they must not forsake church attendance and fellowship.

*"Let us hold fast the confession of our hope without wavering, for He who promised is faithful; and let us consider how to stimulate one another to love and good deeds, **not forsaking our own assembling together**, as is the habit of some, but encouraging one another; and all the more as you see the day drawing near"* (Heb. 10:23–25).

Clear
Command

## Conclusion

In order for there to be ongoing growth and change in the life of a believer who has been living in unrepentant sin, we need to encourage them to be mentored, accountable, discipled, and committed to fellowship in church among God's people. If these actions are not done, then growth and change in the life of a believer once caught in sin will be slow and difficult. They will also run the great risk of falling back into their sinful patterns and lifestyle.

For resources for discipleship, we have written two books on this topic. The first is the main book and the second is the study guide companion.

❖ *Biblical Discipleship: Essential Components for Reaching Spiritual Maturity*

❖ *Biblical Discipleship: Essential Components for Reaching Spiritual Maturity 16 Week Study Guide*

Please visit: ToddMichaelFink.com to see or purchase these books.

# Chapter 22

## Conclusion

## Corrective Church Discipline Gives the Church Power and Blessing

The lack of corrective church discipline today in most Evangelical churches is affecting the level of spiritual depth among many believers. This, in turn, produces Christians who are more susceptible to being hypocrites because their lives don't match their words. It then leads to the diminishing power of the church to speak out against society's sins because Christians are caught up in the very same sins that should be condemned. As a result, the church's ability to fulfill the Great Commission and be a light to the world is sacrificed or damaged.

## Corrective Church Discipline Causes Church Growth

In an article by Crossword.org titled, "10 Things You Should Know About Church Discipline" by Johnathan Leeman, He reveals the following:

> Church discipline was a common practice among churches until the 20th century. In the 19th century, Baptist churches in America excommunicated an average of 2% of their members per year, and yet the growth of these churches outpaced general population growth. Toward the end of the 19th and early 20th century, churches became more interested in reforming society (e.g., temperance movements) than in reforming themselves. The advent of

church marketing in the middle of the 20th century led churches to focus more on product appeal than on holiness. No voices rose up to speak against discipline. Rather, the practice just faded away (see Greg Wills, Democratic Religion)."[36]

Leeman reveals that a lack of church discipline actually causes a church to shrink, instead of growing. I believe this happens for three reasons: (1) a church loses God's blessing (2) mature believers in the church leave because they see God's Word being disobeyed and sinful behavior being taken lightly by leadership, and (3) sin is not viewed as that bad by the church, which in turn, spreads a spirit of disobedience and passivity among the flock.

Leeman goes on to say:

Church discipline ultimately leads to church growth, just as pruning a rose bush leads to more roses. Said another way, church discipline is one aspect of Christian discipleship. Notice that the words "disciple" and "discipline" are etymological cousins. Both words are taken from the realm of education, which involves teaching and correction. Not surprisingly, there's a

---

[36] Johnathan Leeman, https://www.crossway.org/articles/10-things-you-should-know-about-church-discipline/

centuries-old practice of referring to "formative discipline" and "corrective discipline."[37]

John MacArthur also speaks about how exercising church discipline causes a church to grow:

> Nothing guarantees biblical success like church discipline. You read that correctly — when it comes to growing a godly, biblical church, purity must be the first priority.[38]

## Corrective Church Discipline Is a Form of Discipleship

We need to recognize that discipleship is what develops within us spiritual maturity. Without it, we'll be less effective in reaching the world as our lack of example will hinder our message.

Being a disciple of Christ is a call to obey His commands. If we fall into continual sin, then we should expect to be lovingly confronted by mature believers who love us enough to tell us. When the church lovingly confronts sin in its ranks, it is not being hateful or judgmental, but loving.

Discipleship entails both a forward and backward-looking focus. It encourages believers who are right with God to move forward in their journey toward

---

[37] Johnathan Leeman, A Church Discipline Primer, https://www.9marks.org/article/church-discipline-primer/

[38] John MacArthur, Grace to You Blog, February 5, 2013.

spiritual maturity, and it looks backward to seek out believers who are left behind in the process due to their involvement in sin. Corrective church discipline is part of the "seeking out" aspect that rescues believers who are left behind and is an integral part of discipleship. When we overlook corrective church discipline, we overlook a critical element of discipleship.

## Corrective Church Discipline Is Love in Its Truest Sense

God wants the church to cooperate with Him in rescuing a believer living in unrepentant sin and see them restored in their relationship to Him and the church fellowship. If we truly love believers who have fallen into sin, and if we truly believe that sin brings death and destruction, then we will cooperate with God in exercising corrective church discipline so we can rescue and restore fallen believers.

## Closing Thoughts

In this book, we have attempted to let God say what He says regarding the process of corrective church discipline. It's an issue dear to God's heart but severely neglected today by most churches.

God is the one who has raised the issue and spoken about it. It's His topic, and it's His business! Christ talked about it, the Apostle Paul spoke of it, James addressed it, and other New Testament authors dealt with it as well.

We are commanded to preach the whole counsel of God so we shouldn't pick and choose the topics we like and avoid the ones we dislike. However, it's clear today that this vital aspect of God's counsel is largely being neglected and rarely practiced.

Implementing corrective church discipline is love. However, it's sad that the very means God has instituted for rescuing believers living in unrepentant sin from the grips of spiritual death is commonly viewed by many as hate, rather than love. What a tragedy! As a result, the "Intensive Care Unit" of most churches is out of order, and numerous believers are dying spiritual deaths because its doors are closed.

May we, as members of Christ's Church, be faithful in fulfilling the purposes to which we are called. May we be strong and courageous, not putting our finger to the wind and following the crowd regarding corrective church discipline.

Thank you for taking the time to read this book and for caring about this doctrine! You are in the minority. May God richly bless you as you seek to obey Him in all matters and reach your high calling in Christ Jesus!

# Bibliography

Adams, Jay. *Handbook of Church Discipline*. Grand Rapids, Michigan. Zondervan. 1986. 68.

C. S. Lewis Institute. *Sparking a Discipleship Movement in America and Beyond*. cslewisinstitute.org. http://www.cslewisinstitute.org/webfm_send/210. Accessed 08/19/2015.

Cole, Steven J. *Dealing with Sinning Christians: An Overview of Church Discipline*, https://bible.org/article/dealing-sinning-christians-overview-church-discipline-matthew-1815-17-1-corinthians-51-13, accessed 02/18/2019.

Dever, Mark. *Church Discipline: How the Church Protects the Name of Jesus*. Crossway, Wheaton, IL., 2012.

_____. *Nine Marks of a Healthy Church*. Crossway. 2000.

Elliff, Jim, and, Wingerd, Daryl. *Restoring Those Who Fall*. Christian Communicators. www.CCWtoday.org. 2006.

Greco, Fred. *Church Discipline*. https://www.ligonier.org/learn/articles/church-discipline/. Accessed 02/18/2019.

Grudem, Wayne. *Pastoral Leadership for Manhood and Womanhood*. Crossway. 2002.

Hull, Bill. *The Complete Book of Discipleship: On Being and Making Followers of Christ*. The Navigators Reference Library 1. 2014. NavPress. Kindle Edition.

# Bibliography

Jones, Martin Lloyd. *What is an Evangelical?* The Banner of Truth Trust. 1992.

Keathley, Hampton, J. III. *Church Discipline.* Bible.org, https://bible.org/article/church-discipline. Accessed 10/08/2015.

Leeman, Johnathan. Crossway.org. https://www.crossway.org/articles/10-things-you-should-know-about-church-discipline/. Accessed 12/08/2018.

_____. *What are the Standards for Membership?* by Jonathan Leeman. Taken from Church Membership by Jonathan Leeman. 2012, Crossway Books. Wheaton Illinois. 60187, www.crosswaybooks.org.

MacArthur, John. Grace to You. *Church Discipline.* www.gty.org/resources/distinctives/DD02/church-discipline. Accessed 10/08/2015.

_____. *Galatians*, Moody, 1987, p. 57.

_____. *1 Corinthians*, Moody, 1984, p. 125.

_____. *1 Corinthians*, Moody, 1984, p. 127.

_____. Grace to You Blog, February 5, 2013.

_____. Grace to You Newsletter, April 2009, www.gty.org.

Mack, Wayne. *To Be or Not to Be a Church Member.* Calvary Press. www.calvarypress.com. 2004.

Mohler, Albert, R. *The Disappearance of Church Discipline–How Can We Recover? Part One.* 2005. AlbertMohler.com. www.albertmohler.com/2005/05/13/the-disappearance-of-church-discipline-how-can-we-recover-part-one. Accessed 08/21/2015.

Prime, Derek, and, Begg, Alistair. *On Being a Pastor.* Moody Press, 2004.

Robinson, Anthony B. The Renewed Focus on Discipleship: 'Follow Me'. 2007. Christian Century, 124 no 18 S 4 2007. Publication Type: Article. ATLA Religion Database with ATLASerials. Hunter Resource Library. Accessed 12/10/2014.

Schmucker, Matt. *Something Different.* Tabletalk. March 2009. Used by Permission.

Smith, Randy. *Sermon, Severity, Sorrow and Satan.* 2 Corinthians 2:5-11. February 23, 2014. http://jerseygrace.org/sermon/severity-sorrow-and-satan/. Accessed 02/09/2019.

Strauch, Alexander. *Leading with Love.* Lewis and Roth. 2006. Used by Permission.

Thomas, Curtis. *Life in the Body of Christ.* Founders Press, 2006.

Tredgold, Gordon. *7 Truths About Accountability That You Need to Know.* www.inc.com/gordon-tredgold/7-truths-about-accountability-that-you-need-to-kno.html. Accessed 12/15/2018.

Willard, Dallas. *The Great Omission.* 2009-10-13. HarperCollins. Kindle Edition.

# About the Author

Todd M. Fink is founder and director of Go Missions to Mexico Ministries. He received a Bachelor of Theology Degree from Freelandia Bible College (1986-1990), did studies at Western Seminary (1990-1993), received a Master of Theology Degree from Freedom Bible College and Seminary (2012-2013), and received a Ph.D. degree in theology from Trinity Theological Seminary (2015).

He served as youth/associate pastor for 12 years at an Evangelical church in Oregon (1987-1998).

 Todd (Mike) is currently serving as pastor and missionary with Go Missions to Mexico Ministries in Mexico (1998-present) and is also an author, speaker, and teacher. He has a deep passion for God's Word and enjoys helping people understand its eternal truths. He is married to his lovely wife, Letsy Angela, and has four grown children.

# Other Books by Todd M. Fink

*Biblical Discipleship: Essential Components for Reaching Spiritual Maturity*

*Biblical Discipleship: Essential Components for Reaching Spiritual Maturity 16 Week Study Guide*

*Discovering the True Riches of Life*

*Israel: Biblical Sites Travel Guide*

Please visit: ToddMichaelFink.com to see or purchase these books.

## Connect with Todd (Mike)

**Email:** missionstomexico@yahoo.com

**Facebook:** Todd Mike Fink

**Facebook Ministry Page:** Go Missions to Mexico

**Websites:**

- ToddMichaelFink.com
- SelahBookPress.com
- GoMissionsToMexico.com
- HolyLandSite.com
- MinsiteriosCasaDeLuz.com

Made in the USA
Middletown, DE
28 June 2019